Spectrum

Spectrum

An anthology of English varieties for
intermediate and more advanced students

Michael Swan

Cambridge University Press
Cambridge
London   New York   New Rochelle
Melbourne   Sydney

Published by the Press Syndicate of the University of Cambridge
The Pitt Building, Trumpington Street, Cambridge CB2 IRP
32 East 57th Street New York, NY 10022, USA
296 Beaconsfield Parade, Middle Park, Melbourne 3206, Australia

First published 1978
Reprinted 1979, 1980

Designed by Peter Ducker

Printed in Great Britain
at the Alden Press, Oxford

ISBN 0 521 21622 2

To Adrian
most encouraging of editors

Acknowledgements

The editor and publishers are grateful to the authors, publishers and others who have given permission for the use of copyright material identified in the text. It has not been possible to identify the sources of all the material used and in such cases the publishers would welcome information from copyright owners.

The extract from *Intimate Behaviour* by Desmond Morris is used by permission of Jonathan Cape; the extracts from the Nanette Newman books are by permission of Collins Publishers and Nanette Newman; the Osbert Lancaster cartoon from *Signs of the Times* is by permission of John Murray; the passages from *Children's Letters to God* by Eric Marshall and Stuart Hemple, published by Collins & Sons Co. Ltd, are by permission of A. D. Peters & Co. Ltd; the material from the *Australasian Express* is by permission; the extract from *The Young Meteors* is by permission of Curtis Brown Ltd on behalf of Jonathan Aitken; the passage from Aldous Huxley's *Point Counter Point* is by permission of Mrs Laura Huxley and Chatto & Windus Ltd; all material from *The Observer* is by permission; all material from the *Daily Mirror* is © Syndication International Ltd; the *Punch* cartoons are reproduced by permission of *Punch*; the 'Currency Rates' are from *International Herald Tribune* 1976; the Ronald Searle drawings are printed by permission of Hope Leresche & Sayle, © 1956 by Ronald Searle, first published in *Merry England* and © from *The Female Approach* and © 1948 from *Hurrah for St Trinian's*; the Ashleigh Brilliant Pot-Shots are by permission; the Giles cartoons are reproduced by permission of London Express News and Feature Services; 'What Did you Learn in School Today?' by Tom Paxton is by permission of Harmony Music Ltd; the extract from *Eat It* is by permission of Bellerophon Books; the material from *Laughter in a Damp Climate* by Eric Linfield and Egon Larsen is by permission of Barrie & Jenkins; the extract from *The Isle of Skye* is by permission of Photo Precision Ltd, St Ives, Huntingdon, Cambs.; the extracts from David Daiches' *Scotch Whisky*, *Honor Blackman's Book of Self-Defence* and George Mikes' *How to Be an Alien* are by permission of Andre Deutsch; the extract on whisky is from an advertisement for Teacher's Highland Cream Scotch Whisky; the extract on the pub is by permission of J. Hannon & Co. (Publishers) Oxford; the material from *The Frying Pan*, published by

permission of Penguin Books; 'Old age' by J. B. Priestley published by *The Times* is by permission of A. D. Peters & Co. Ltd; Jenny Joseph's poem is published by Dent.

Introduction

Written English is not just literature, newspaper reports and magazine articles. During a typical day our eyes take in an enormous variety of written messages: business letters, bills, advertisements, notices, personal letters, train timetables, parking tickets, bank statements, political slogans, book-jackets, road-signs, shopping lists, graffiti, the labels on beer-bottles . . . the list is endless.

One purpose of this book is simply to provide examples of this variety. The student of English abroad can find plenty of 'good writing' in his textbooks, but it is not always so easy for him to get the taste of practical everyday communication in English. It is certainly a fine thing to study Hemingway's prose style or Galbraith's views on economics, but it can also be interesting to see how a London estate agent advertises a house for sale, or what kinds of thing English children find in their comics. The texts reproduced here have therefore been chosen deliberately in order to include as many kinds of communication as possible. They differ widely in subject-matter, purpose, style and visual presentation. Not all of them are in 'standard' English, nor are they all of British or American origin. Although the emphasis is on written communication, there are also a number of transcriptions of spoken language.

A second purpose – equally important – is to entertain, amuse, inform, surprise, move and occasionally shock the reader. As far as possible, I have chosen texts not only because they illustrate certain types of communication, but also because they have some interest in themselves, either alone or in combination with the texts that come before and after them. Each extract is linked with the next by some kind of association (for instance, similarity of subject-matter or style). The book has the same loose organization as a 'train of thought', and wanders, not very systematically, over perhaps forty or fifty topics. There is no need to start at the beginning or read from left to right: the book is meant to be picked up, dipped into, put down, and (I hope) picked up again later. Brief vocabulary explanations are provided as a quick aid to reading; they should not of course be regarded as complete explanations of the meaning or use of the words explained.

I have tried to provide a reasonably balanced selection of subjects and attitudes, so that the book should contain something for everybody. Obviously, any collection of this kind is personal, and must to some extent reflect the editor's tastes, interests, and political and social concerns. No one person can be expected to share all my likes, dislikes and enthusiasms: I hope at least that most readers will enjoy most of the texts.

A number of people have helped me with suggestions, advice and criticism: I should like to thank all of them, and particularly H. A. Swan, Claire Boasson, Stuart Hagger and my wife.

Note for teachers

A collection of short authentic texts like this is obviously particularly suitable for extensive reading practice outside the classroom. However, it can also be used as a basis for various kinds of classwork. Examples of possible activities are:

Class discussion: a text or group of texts can be used as a jumping-off point for discussion of the writers' ideas and attitudes.

Lecturettes: individual students can each choose a text and tell the rest of the class about their reactions to it.

Vocabulary study: students can work intensively on the words and expressions contained in a text, distinguishing (with the teacher's guidance) between items that are useful for recognition only and items that can become part of their active vocabulary.

Guided composition: students can practise writing in the same style as the text, or using the vocabulary of the text to express their own ideas on the subject.

Stylistic analysis: a class can discuss the style of a particular passage, or compare the styles of different texts on the same subject.

Background study: texts can provide a useful basis for discussion of British and American cultural attitudes, institutions, etc.

Spectrum

XA 843996 *PAS 11393*

1 & 2 ELIZ. 2 CH. 20

CERTIFICATE OF BIRTH

Name and Surname *albert Williams*

Sex *Boy*

Date of Birth *Fifth December 1906*

Place of Birth { Registration *Islington* / District / Sub-district *Islington, South East* }

Certified to have been compiled from records in the custody of the Registrar General. Given at the General Register Office, Somerset House, London, under the Seal of the said Office, the *22nd* day of *January* 1958.

CAUTION :—*Any person who (1) falsifies any of the particulars on this certificate, or (2) uses a falsified certificate as true knowing it to be false, is liable to prosecution.*

15/284/338

The experience of birth

Towards the end of pregnancy, in the last three months before birth, the baby is also capable of hearing. There is still nothing to see, taste or smell, but things that go bump in the night of the womb can be clearly detected. If a loud, sharp noise is made near to the mother's belly, it startles the baby inside and makes it jump. The movement can easily be recorded by sensitive instruments and may even be strong enough for the mother to feel it herself. This means that during this period before birth the baby is undoubtedly capable of hearing the steady thump of the maternal heartbeat, 72 times every minute. It will become imprinted as the major sound-signal of life in the womb.

These, then, are our first real experiences of life – floating in a warm fluid, curling inside a total embrace, swaying to the undulations of the moving body and hearing the beat of the pulsing heart. Our prolonged exposure to these sensations in the absence of other, competing stimuli leaves a lasting impression on our brains, an impression that spells security, comfort and passivity.

This intra-uterine bliss is then rudely and rapidly shattered by what must be one of the most traumatic experiences in our entire lives – the act of being born. The uterus, in a matter of hours, is transformed from a cosy nest into a straining, squeezing sac of muscle, the largest and most powerful muscle in the whole human body, athlete's arms included. The lazy embrace that became a snug hug now becomes a crushing constriction. The newly delivered baby displays, not a happy, welcoming grin, but the strained, tightly contorted facial expressions of a desperate torture victim. Its cries, which are such sweet music to the anxiously waiting parents, are in reality nothing short of the wild screams of blind panic, as it is exposed to the sudden loss of intimate body contact.

At the moment of birth the baby appears floppy, like soft wet rubber, but almost at once it makes a gasping action and takes its first breath. Then, five to six seconds later, it starts to cry. Its head, legs and arms begin to move about with increasing intensity and for the next thirty minutes it continues to protest in irregular outbursts of limb-thrashing, grasping, grimacing and screaming, after which it usually subsides exhausted into a long sleep.

(Desmond Morris, *Intimate Behaviour*)

go bump: make a noise
womb: place where a baby grows inside the mother's body
belly: abdomen, lower part of the body
imprinted: fixed in the memory for ever
fluid: liquid
curling: lying rolled up, not straight
swaying: moving from side to side
undulations: rising and falling movements
stimuli: (plural of *stimulus*) things for the brain to pay attention to
intra-uterine: inside the womb
traumatic: causing an unforgettable shock
uterus: womb
snug hug: close, comfortable embrace
panic: uncontrolled terror
floppy: not stiff, tending to hang loosely
limb-thrashing: making violent movements with its arms and legs
grimacing: twisting its face into expressions of pain or anger

I saw a book once with all drawings in it about falling in love and I think you have to have eggs.

Vera aged 5

IF a baby dropz out of your tummy When your zhopping You muzt ring the police.

Deborah aged 6

Once you've had a baby you cant put it back.

Andrea aged 6

MY CAT HATES BABIES BECAUSE. THEY DRINK HIS MILK

Cathy aged 6

4

To get a vote you have to kiss old women and babies and that spreads deseese

Karina aged 7

(Collected by Nanette Newman)

tummy: children's word for stomach
deseese: mis-spelling of disease

'Oh, we're enjoying every minute of it – he's bitten the Tory, been sick over the Socialist, and now I can hardly wait to see what he's going to do to the Liberal!'

Osbert Lancaster

OXFORD CITY COUNCIL — EAST WARD BY-ELECTION

from

JEAN MATTHEWS

your Conservative candidate

37 Stratford Street
Oxford
Tel.No. 49286

Dear Elector,

Having always lived in or near East Oxford, I hope that you will vote for me on Thursday, 28th October, to represent you on the City Council.

I attended St Faith's School. I am married and have a teenage daughter. I work part-time as an Assistant in the University Laboratories. I have always supported local organisations which help people in need, particularly the disabled. I am a founder member of the British Heart Foundation in Oxford.

In the present financial situation essential services must come first. Conservatives believe in not spending more than the ratepayers can afford. But, with my Conservative colleagues, I want more positive action to preserve the character of this part of the City

* More information given to *all* householders about improvement grants
* A sensible traffic management scheme
* A more efficient street cleansing service
* Existing open spaces to be retained for the benefit of residents
* That part of Meadow Lane, leading to the New School to be improved to cycle-track standard
* Residents' car-parking schemes to be extended to East Oxford
* Continued pressure for more post box and telephone facilities, particularly in Southfield Park
* Sheltered housing for the elderly — like Rosemary Court — so that East Oxford people do not have to leave their friends when they move

Financial restraints are now being imposed on the City Council all the time. As your Councillor I would

* work, with my fellow Conservative councillors, to get these things done within the restrictions imposed by the Government
* always be ready to see and talk to residents and hold surgeries

I therefore ask you to help me to make East Oxford a place where people are happy to live, and to vote for me next Thursday.

Kind regards,

Jean Matthews

**VOTE
CONSERVATIVE**

MATTHEWS	**X**

**THURSDAY
28th OCTOBER**

If you need a car to take you to vote ring 46792/44027

A MESSAGE from Fred Kane and Sheila Zinkin, the East Ward Councillors: "We are looking forward to Jean Matthews joining us on the Council. She is a really first-rate candidate. Do support her — and help us to get on with the job."

Printed by Holywell Press, Alfred Street, Oxford and published by S.R.Chaplin, Frewin Court, Cornmarket, Oxford

ward: local government district
by-election: election made necessary by death or retirement of a Councillor or M.P.
the disabled: people who cannot use their arms or legs properly (e.g. because of accidents)
ratepayers: rates are local government taxes on people who occupy houses or flats
improvement grants: money paid to people to help them modernize their homes
surgeries: (here) meetings at which people with problems can talk to their Councillor

6

Santa Claus: Father Christmas

Ronald Searle

'It is not my intention to work you up
into a state of mass hysteria...'

7

Great men

Shakespeare, in the familiar lines, divided great men into three classes: those born great, those who achieve greatness, and those who have greatness thrust upon them. It never occurred to him to mention those who hire public relations experts and press secretaries to make themselves look great.

Daniel Boorstin

thrust: pushed, forced

Nixon on TV

[Richard Nixon hired a team of public relations experts to help him with the 1968 presidential election. They presented Nixon to the nation in a series of very carefully prepared television shows. Here is how one of the team described the purpose of the broadcasts.]

Let's face it, a lot of people think Nixon is dull. Think he's a bore, a pain in the ass. They look at him as the kind of kid who always carried a bookbag. Who was forty-two years old the day he was born. They figure other kids got footballs for Christmas, Nixon got briefcases and he loved it. He'd always have his homework done and he'd never let you copy. Now you put him on television, you've got a problem right away. He's a funny-looking guy. He looks like somebody hung him in a closet overnight and he jumps out in the morning with his suit all bunched up and starts running around saying 'I want to be President'. I mean this is how he strikes some people. That's why these shows are important. To make them forget all that.

(Joe McGinniss, *The Selling of the President 1968*)

pain in the ass: vulgar expression meaning a boring or annoying person
figure: (spoken American) think
briefcases: cases for carrying papers
closet: (American) cupboard

Monique strips for MPs

CANBERRA: A party last week for a group of Liberal MPs was called off shortly after a stripper jumped out of a cake and took her clothes off.

The strip occurred in Parliament House in front of Liberal MPs attending a party for members elected in 1966.

The incident drew questions in Parliament and a demand for action from Opposition MPs.

About 25 Liberals, including 5 Cabinet Ministers, were at the party being held in the members' dining room.

The 25-year-old stripper, known only as Monique, leapt from a giant birthday cake and shouted "Happy Anniversary". She switched on a portable cassette and began a go-go dance.

But the delight on the members faces turned to horror when the girl peeled off her bra and danced topless.

In the best of Liberal tradition, the members present agreed to a vow of silence over the issue, but the story was leaked by someone who had drifted into the room at the time of the incident and left undetected.

Parliamentary reporters established that the girl is the wife of a local businessman who had given his permission for the strip.

It is also believed that the girl did not leave Parliament House until 2.15 am — almost three hours after the performance.

(*Australasian Express*)

called off: cancelled
bra: brassière (piece of underclothing that holds the breasts)
vow: promise
issue: matter, question
leaked: made public
drifted: wandered

Roller chaos

MELBOURNE — More than 200 girls were treated by ambulance officers at the Bay City Rollers concert in Melbourne last week.

Most were carried sobbing and screaming out of the hall by the officers.

After the show, police called in extra cars when about 300 fans, thinking the group was still at the hall, charged down Rosslyn Street.

Police linked arms along one side of the street while others in a courtesy car appealed to the girls to go home.

When the manager's car arrived, the girls swarmed around it, believing it had come for the group.

Police took over an hour to clear the area after the show had finished.

Bouncers lifted unconscious girls onto the stage and carried them through back doors where a team of St John Ambulance officers were waiting to treat them.

Members of the group and the compere, Ian Meldrum, shouted appeals over the microphones for the girls to keep quiet.

The road behind the hall looked like a battlefield.

Ambulance men and women helpers worked from four vehicles, treating girls who had passed out.

The show was stopped a second time when fans at the rear of the hall pushed forward, crushing those in front against the stage.

Police and officials linked arms but were unable to stop the crowd.

(*Australasian Express*)

Bay City Rollers: a group of pop musicians
sobbing: crying
fans: admirers of the group
linked: joined
swarmed: crowded
bouncers: people responsible for keeping order at dances, pop concerts, etc.
compere: announcer
passed out: fainted

NORMAL EVENT

Recently I read an article about the behaviour of teenagers at pop concerts. Words like "uncontrollable," and "dreadful," were used to describe the fans' behaviour — but I think this is most unfair.

In my experience, pop concerts have been fantastic; there has never been any trouble or violence, and even though some girls faint, critics don't seem to understand that this is due to pure emotion.

I am sure that a lot of other "Jackie" readers feel the same way as I do. So come on, all you critics — pop concerts are normal, enjoyable events and not nearly as terrible as you think!

**A Mud Fan,
Skelmersdale,
Lancs.**

(Letter in *Jackie*, a girls' magazine)

A Mud Fan: an admirer of the pop group called 'Mud'

Peter Townshend

Peter Townshend, 23, grammar school (three A-levels) and Ealing Art College, makes £60,000 a year as guitarist of The Who.

Being a modern pop star is a sort of way of being intellectual without being intellectual. Intelligence is useful, but you can easily get snowed under by the lava of publicity, and hysteria, and screaming women. It's so easy, too. I've fulfilled my wildest dreams already, and I'm sure I'm going to fulfil my even wilder dreams in the future, but it's a bit of a hollow triumph. I make a lot of money, but I'm not all that happy.

(Jonathan Aitken, *The Young Meteors*)

The Who: a pop group
snowed under: buried
hollow: empty

Work gives them the comfortable illusion of existing, even of being important. If they stopped working, they'd realize they simply weren't there at all, most of them. Just holes in the air, that's all.

Aldous Huxley

What do you do, Daddy?

A young boy asks his father, 'What do you do, Daddy?' Here is how the father *might* answer: 'I struggle with crowds, traffic jams and parking problems for about an hour. I talk a great deal on the telephone to people I hardly know. I dictate to a secretary and then proof-read what she types. I have all sorts of meetings with people I don't know very well or like very much. I eat lunch in a big hurry and can't taste or remember what I've eaten. I hurry, hurry, hurry. I spend my time in very functional offices with very functional furniture, and I never look at the weather or sky or people passing by. I talk but I don't sing or dance or touch people. I spend the last hour, all alone, struggling with crowds, traffic and parking.' Now this same father might also answer: 'I am a lawyer. I help people and businesses to solve their problems. I help everybody to know the rules that we all have to live by, and to get along according to these rules.'

Both answers are true. Why is the first truth less recognized than the second?

. . . It might be said that we are trained to be aware of the goal of our activities, but not to be aware of what is actually happening. What are we doing? Going from New York to San Francisco. Ask again. Sitting five abreast, bored and anxious, re-reading the airlines brochure, cramped, isolated, seeing and thinking nothing.

(Charles Reich, *The Greening of America*)

proof-read: check for mistakes
functional: designed to be useful rather than beautiful
goal: purpose
five abreast: in rows of five
cramped: without enough room to move

Two happy workers

[Extracts from interviews in which people were asked how they liked their work.]

1. A teacher

'I'm from Missouri. I'm a teacher of French to 13-year-olds in a high school.'

How do you like your work?

'I love it. I love the relationship between myself and the students. At that age the student is just developing his own ideas about the world and about the people around him; it's fascinating to watch and take part in the process.'

Do you think that work takes too much of your time?

'Well, in teaching you can spend 24 hours a day in preparation and research – I always wish I had four or five more hours a day, because I have children and I'm involved with *their* activities at the same time.'

Do you think that people work very hard in the US?

'Yes, I feel that most people are very conscientious and put a high value on their work. Those that just put in the time clock-watching, waiting to go home – they probably don't feel really involved and perhaps they're dissatisfied.'

Why do you think work is so highly valued?

'Well, first of all people want money in order to improve their standard of living. But in the States, particularly in the last 5–10 years, people have become more concerned with how they can serve, how they can contribute to their society.'

2. A checker in a car factory

How do you like your job?

'Beautiful. I sit down and do nothing all day.'

Don't you like work?

'No, I detest it. I always have and I always will.'

Why?

'I'm one of those awkward individuals who don't see the point in expending a lot of effort in order to make the boss richer. I believe in getting the maximum possible for the minimum of effort – and believe me, that is exactly what I do.'

Do you think that people work too much in general?

'Definitely. Undeniably.'

are conscientious: have a strong sense of duty
detest: hate
awkward: unco-operative
undeniably: unquestionably

Domestic Jobs

**IF YOU NEED WORK
WE NEED YOU**

£3.00 + fares for 4-hour sessions, morning or afternoon. Central or North-West London.
580 1949.

EARN £2.50
every three hours plus 20p towards fares
PROBLEM LTD
All sorts of jobs; you could scrub floors one day and run a message to Paris the next. Work when you want—keep all you earn. No agency commission—as much work as you want.
For details ring
828 4077.

NO HASSLE AND GOOD BREAD
Living NW/Central districts

Work mornings or afternoons, all day if you can get it together, cleaning private houses.
Paid daily.
Top rates plus fares.
624 9774.

● **'Short of money'.** Earn £5 per day, plus your fares. Domestic cleaning in N London. Ring Halien, 794 2256.
● **NEED MORE MONEY** Part-time day work available for responsible young people. £6 daily plus fares. LONDON DOMESTICS LTD. 584 0161.
● **BABYSITTERS AND DAY NANNIES WANTED.** Spare time work for nurses, teachers etc. Experience with small babies essential. Childminders 01-487 4578.
● **Cleaning work available** for people living North, North West and Central London. Top rates plus fares. 624 4747/ 7319.

(Advertisements in *Time Out*)

hassle: (slang) difficulty, unpleasantness
bread: (slang) money
get it together: (slang) organize yourself
rates: payments

Sent away to service

[The speaker is recalling her childhood in the 'Fenland' – a low-lying, marshy area in eastern Cambridgeshire and Lincolnshire. Her speech is characteristic of the dialect of the region.]

It were nothing for a girl to be sent away to service when she were eleven year old. This meant leaving the family as she had never been parted from for a day in her life before, and going to some place miles away to be treated like something as ha'n't got as much sense or feeling as a dog. I'm got nothing against girls going into good service. In my opinion, good service in a properly run big house were a wonderful training for a lot o' girls who never would ha' seen anything different all the days o' their lives if they ha'n't a-gone. It were better than working on the land, then, and if it still existed now, I reckon I'd rather see any o' my daughters be a good housemaid or a well-trained parlourmaid than a dolled-up shop assistant or a factory worker. But folks are too proud to work for other folks, now, even if it's to their own advantage, though as far as I can see you are still working for other folks, whatever you're a-doing. Such gals as us from the fen di'n't get 'good' service though, not till we'd learnt a good deal the hard way. Big houses di'n't want little girls of eleven, even as kitchen maids, so the first few years 'ad to be put in somewhere else, afore you got even that amount o' promotion. Big houses expected good service, but you got good treatment in return. It wern't like that at the sort o' place my friends had to go to. Mostly they went to the farmers's houses within ten or twenty mile from where they'd been born. These farmers were a jumped up, proud lot who di'n't know how to treat the people who worked for 'em. They took advantage o' the poor peoples' need to get their girls off their hands to get little slaves for nearly nothing. The conditions were terrible.

(Sybil Marshall, *Fenland Chronicle*)

service: the life and work of a servant
it were, she were: (dialect) it was, she was
as she had never been parted from: (dialect) that she had . . .
ha'n't: (dialect) hadn't
I'm got: (dialect) I've got
a-gone, a-doing: (dialect) gone, doing
dolled-up: wearing make-up and fashionable clothes
gals: (dialect) girls
the fen: a flat, wet region of Cambridgeshire and Lincolnshire
learnt . . . the hard way: learnt from experience
afore: (dialect) before
a jumped up . . . lot: people who had got rich quickly

Utopian conditions

[This is a copy of office rules issued by an Australian firm of merchants and ships' chandlers in the year 1852.]

1. Godliness, Cleanliness and Punctuality are the necessities of a good business.

2. On the recommendation of the Governor of this Colony, this firm has reduced the hours of work, and the Clerical Staff will now have to be present between the hours of 7.00 a.m. and 6.00 p.m. on weekdays. The Sabbath is for Worship, but should any Man-of-War or other vessel require victualling, the Clerical Staff will work on the Sabbath.

3. Daily Prayers will be held each morning in the Main Office. The Clerical Staff will be present.

4. Clothing must be of a sober nature. The Clerical Staff will not disport themselves in raiments of bright colours, nor will they wear hose, unless in good repair.

5. Overshoes and Top coats may not be worn in the office but Neck scarves and Head-wear may be worn in inclement weather.

6. A stove is provided for the benefit of the Clerical Staff. Coal and Wood must be kept in the locker. It is recommended that each member of the Clerical Staff brings four pounds of coal each day, during cold weather.

7. No Member of the Clerical Staff may leave the room without permission from Mr. Ryder. The calls of nature are permitted, and the Clerical Staff may use the garden below the second gate. This area must be kept in good order.

8. No talking allowed during business hours.

9. The craving for tobacco, wines or spirits is a human weakness, and, as such, is forbidden to all members of the Clerical Staff.

10. Now that the hours of business have been drastically reduced the partaking of food is allowed between 11.30 a.m. and noon, but the work will not, on any account, cease.

11. Members of the Clerical Staff will provide their own pens. A new sharpener is available, on application to Mr. Ryder.

12. Mr. Ryder will nominate a Senior Clerk to be responsible for the cleanliness of the Main Office and the Private Office, and all boys and juniors will report to him 40 minutes before Prayers, and will remain after closing hours for similar work. Brushes, Brooms, Scrubbers and Soap are provided by the owners.

13. The New Increased Weekly Wages are as hereunder detailed:

    Junior Boys . . . . 1s. 4d.
    Boys . . . . 2s. 1d.

Juniors	4s. 8d.
Junior Clerks	8s. 7d.
Clerks	10s. 9d.
Senior Clerks (after 15 years with the owners)	21s. 0d.

The owners hereby recognize the generosity of the new labour laws, but will expect a great rise in output of work to compensate for these near Utopian conditions.

ships' chandlers: ships' suppliers
the clerical staff: the clerks, secretaries, etc.
the Sabbath: Sunday
worship: attending religious services
man-of-war: warship
vessel: ship
victualling: supplying
disport themselves in raiments of bright colours: wear brightly coloured clothes
hose: stockings or socks
the calls of nature: going to the lavatory
craving: strong desire
partaking: eating

Feiffer

17

My dad works at being a striker and when I grow up I shall work there as well

---

Incomes 1976

Some typical incomes in 1976 Britain, including overtime in several instances. As with all examples of earnings, those doing these particular jobs who receive less will complain that they aren't so lucky, and those who receive more will say nothing. But they are all realistic before-tax figures :—

	£
Chairman of large public company	40.000
Consultant physician in provinces with private practice	17,000
Solicitor in partnership	15,000
Bank manager	10,000
General practitioner	10,000
Comprehensive school headmaster	8,500
Manager of small engineering works	6,000
BBC radio announcer	5,500
Machine-tool operator	4,500
London dustman	3,900
London bus driver	3,800
Milkman	3,100
Reporter on local newspaper	3,000
Man sweeping factory floor	3,000
Lavatory attendant	2,900

(*The Observer Review*)

overtime: payment for working extra hours
consultant physician: specialist doctor
with private practice: not working for the National Health Service
general practitioner: non–specialist doctor

HOW AN ACCOUNT WORKS

Broadly, there are two kinds of bank account–cheque and deposit. The cheque (or current) account is normally used where fairly frequent incomings and outgoings are anticipated. The deposit account, on the other hand, is really a savings account. As such, the money in it earns interest.

Since you are likely to be needing the service on a day-to-day or

week-to-week basis, a cheque account would probably be the most suitable. This is a simple method of banking which enables you to buy goods and services with cheques instead of cash. You can also, of course, pay money into the account by cheque or cash. When you make out a cheque to a person or a company, it is paid by them into their account at their bank. From there the cheque is passed to the 'inter-bank clearing system' and then sent back to your branch where the amount is subtracted from your account.

That, basically, is it.

(From an information pamphlet for students issued by Barclay's Bank)

"Gloria, the traveller's cheques! Throw out the traveller's cheques!"

Daily Mirror

19

ON A ROAD TO RUIN

YOU are more than fifty-two pence worse off today than you were at the weekend.

That's what the latest crash in the pound's value abroad means to every family in Britain. We are so dependent on imported food, fuel, raw materials and other goods that shop prices must go up.

Economists calculate that each one per cent drop in the pound's value adds 13p to the cost of living for the average family each week.

Since the weekend the pound has plunged by a terrifying 4 per cent, which means 52p on your future weekly housekeeping.

That's not all.

Britain's foreign debts are now more than 15,800 million dollars—which has to be repaid in whatever currency it was borrowed originally.

At exchange rates ruling last weekend, the debt totalled £9,231 millions.

But now the pound is worth so much less, we will have to repay the equivalent of £9,647 millions—an increase of £416 millions

The increase alone works out at an extra £7·42, for every man woman and child in Britain.

The worst thing about our present situation is that we are now on a treadmill to disaster.

The pound is falling because foreigners have no confidence in Britain.

They have no confidence in us because we are up to our neck in debt abroad, and our exports suffer from the handicap of a rate of inflation 75 per cent higher than that of our foreign competitors.

The falling pound makes the inflation worse, by pushing up the cost of imports, and forcing us to borrow more.

Which causes the next run on sterling.

(John Husband, *Daily Mirror*, 29 September 1976)

worse off: poorer
raw materials: minerals, etc., needed by manufacturers
plunged: gone down very fast
treadmill: originally a kind of mill driven by people walking on a wheel; the writer means that we are on a circular track from which there is no escape
handicap: disadvantage
run on sterling: rush to sell sterling

Sterling exchange rates 25 October 1977

New York	$1·7743–7747
Montreal	$1·9755–9765
Amsterdam	4·30$\frac{3}{4}$–31$\frac{3}{4}$ fl
Brussels	62·55–65 f
Copenhagen	10·80$\frac{1}{4}$–81$\frac{1}{4}$ k
Frankfurt	4·01$\frac{1}{4}$–02$\frac{1}{4}$ m
Lisbon	71·85–72·05 e
Madrid	148·35–45 p
Milan	1561–62 lr
Oslo	9·69$\frac{1}{2}$–70$\frac{1}{2}$ k
Paris	8·59–60 f
Stockholm	8·48$\frac{1}{2}$–49$\frac{1}{2}$ k
Tokyo	447–49 y
Vienna	28·60–70 sch
Zurich	3·96$\frac{1}{4}$–97$\frac{1}{4}$ f

Pound rallies after Treasury plans to borrow $3,900m maximum from IMF

(Headline in *The Times*, 30 September 1976)

rallies: becomes stronger
Treasury: the British finance ministry
IMF: the International Monetary Fund

No Saturday post?

Mr Tom Jackson, secretary of the Union of Post Office Workers, has revealed that his members, eager for a five-day week, wish to stop the Saturday mail. "If," he said, "our members decided on no Saturday work, not only would the Saturday letter delivery disappear but also parcels and the collection and onward transmission of mail on Saturday." This, he added rather unnecessarily, would plunge letter and parcel services into chaos at the beginning of each week.

Well, even I can see that. I mean, if no letters are delivered, let alone collected on Saturday, what's going to happen on Monday? Okay, I'll tell you. The Post Office will be so busy sorting out the weekend mail that it won't be able to start delivering Saturday's letters until Tuesday. And on Tuesday all Monday's letters will arrive, gumming up the works so effectively that there won't be another delivery until Thursday.

And even as they're sorting out Monday's mail on Wednesday, all Tuesday's letters will be pouring in, too, and since Friday will be devoted to sorting that lot and there's no delivery on Saturday, why there'll be no possibility of delivering Tuesday's letters until Monday and naturally they can't do that because, by Monday, they'll have also collected Saturday's post and this, added to Wednesday's, Thursday's and Friday's, will give the Post Office workers so much to do that they won't even be able to consider delivering any mail until Saturday at the earliest and, as we all know, there won't be a post on Saturday.

While all this is going on, Sir William will be examining the books and concluding that, as a result of paying postmen the same money for a five-day week as they used to get for a 5½-day week, the Post Office is losing even more money than it did before the 6p post went up to 10p and therefore, in the interests of efficiency and making a profit, he will have to ask reluctantly for an increase in the price of a first-class stamp to 15p.

(Barry Norman, *The Guardian*)

gumming up the works: blocking the machinery
Sir William: Sir William Ryland, the Postmaster General at the time the article was written
examining the books: looking at the accounts
reluctantly: unwillingly

What I wanted
to say was...

I LOVED the weekend post, I'm lost without it; if the Post Office does bring it back next spring I'll be the first to rejoice. But there's no denying that not being able to bung a letter in the post over the weekend has kept me out of an awful lot of trouble—as a simple contrast between the letters I write first and the ones I finally send will show.

Dear Matilda,

Thanks for your letter, which only arrived this morning. I do see it would be simplest if you left the children with us while you go to your friend's wedding and on to a meal and a show; but I don't honestly think we can manage it. Last time you came, Nigel broke a clock that cost 20 quid to repair; we were on our feet every 50 seconds trying to stop Rosemary falling downstairs, since you let her crawl round regardless; and the cats didn't come back for three days. The thought that Sam who that time was at least lashed into a carry-cot, is now old enough to crash round on his own two feet inclines me to think that, if you really want to spend a jolly day in London, you should dump them on the steps of the nearest police station, re-claiming them (if you feel up to it) later. An open, friendly and permissive style of child-rearing may well ensure that children will go happily to other people; but the reverse, I'm afraid, is not the case.

Dear Matilda,

What a shame! I'm so sorry, I'm afraid we'll be away that weekend. And as we've fixed to have the builders in while we're away, I don't think we can really even offer you a bed. It would have been so nice to see you—next time perhaps.

(Katherine Whitehorn, *The Observer*)

bung: (slang) put, throw
20 quid: (slang) £20
regardless: without thinking about the consequences
lashed: tied
dump them: (slang) put them down
up to it: strong enough
child-rearing: bringing up children

Yours sincerely

Yours faithfully

Ronald Searle

A Christmas letter

[This is a copy of a duplicated letter sent out by an American family at Christmas to all their friends and acquaintances.]

December 1974

Merry Christmas Everyone!!

That year has finally arrived when the task of getting all
five of us together with clean faces, hair, etc, is beyond
my time and energies. I hate to give up on a picture.
We are all well and busy, however, and hopefully look about
the same as last year.

Phil and I are deeply involved in building moderately priced
rental housing for our older citizens. We've formed a non-
profit corporation, have an option on 25 acres and plan to
borrow about 900,000 dollars from the Farmers Home Adminis-
tration and build about 40 apartments in a cluster development.
This involved a drastic change in our zoning ordinances. It
takes a lot of time, but has met very favourable reception
and is an exciting and rewarding project.

Last May we took the girls out of school and Phil's folks
took us to climb the Grand Canyon. That was a beautiful trip.
Mary, Sue, Phil and Jim climbed down, stayed overnight and out
the next day. Ann was broken hearted not to go down, but we
all felt she was too carefree at 9 yrs to have enough fear of
a fall. A man had died the week before and I knew I couldn't
watch her for two days without several heart attacks. We
took a plane ride through it instead.

The girls are doing beautifully in school and we are enjoying
them so much at these ages of 9, 12 and 14. Daily challenges,
but lots of fun and laughs too. Mary is dating the quarterback on the Milford football team, so is suddenly in the
social swing sooner than we were prepared for it. But the
boy is delightful as are all of her girl friends. She's
playing tennis and also going out for the ski team. Sue is
in our gorgeous new middle school and loves it. Got all A's
and is doing gymnastics, ballet and basketball. Annie spends
most of her time keeping ahead of the class in math, doing
'projects' and loving our year-old yellow Labrador.

My mother, after a September hospital stay, is doing very
well, - she and my father have even joined our Racquet and
Health Club, and they exercise and swim.

We all send you our best and hope that you have Happy Holidays
and a prosperous New Year.

Sally, Phil, Mary, Sue and Ann

I hate to give up on a picture: normally the family sent out a photograph of themselves
with their Christmas message, but this year it was too difficult to organize
option: the right to buy
acre: about 4,000 square metres
cluster development: group of houses built close together
zoning ordinances: laws about where various kinds of building are and are not allowed
Mary is dating the quarterback: she's his girlfriend
quarterback: a position in an American football team
going out for the ski team: trying to get into the team
gorgeous: (conversational) beautiful
A's: top marks for school work
Labrador: a kind of dog

I'M WRITING
TO TELL YOU
I HAVE NOTHING TO SAY

Ashleigh
Brilliant

A love letter

[This was written by a young teacher to his French girlfriend, several years ago.]

Friday.

My little Teddy,
Are you really 21 and completely grown-up? I can see your face as I write, sleep in yours eyes and a soft smile on your lips. But this is only one of your facets - why should I think of it first? We know, of course.
I am deeply concerned of

your mother's poor health, and although you have shown me a philosophical attitude to her illness, you must know that I will be ready if you ever need me — remember this Françoise.

When your bus passed from view I drove to Wanstead; the journey took only 35 minutes but I did everything automatically. Blanche and I chatted to Hilary, but I was glad to go to bed — although I soon found I had too much room.

These last three days have been hectic — I did not 'wash-up' Tuesday's dishes until tonight. By working very late at school (10 & 8.30 p.m), I was able to allay my lonliness for you and return sufficiently tired to sleep quickly. After this evening's meal

I dozed-off in an armchair until 8 p.m., so you'll not read this until Monday.

Empty of conversation but thinking more of you than I intended.

Goodnight my Teddy

facets: parts of a person's character
concerned of: a slip of the pen – he means *concerned about*
hectic: very hurried and busy
dozed-off: half slept

My thoughts

I sometimes wonder what my mind is like inside, often I fancy that it is like this. I feel as if my mind goes round and round like the earth and if my lessons make me think hard it begins to spin. In my other class it was getting all stodgy and still and lumpy and rusty. I feel as if there is a ball in my mind and it is divided into pieces – each piece stands for a different mood. The ball turns every now and then and that's what makes me change moods. I have my learning mood, my goodlooks mood, my happy mood, my loose-end mood and my grumpy mood, my missrable mood, my thoughtful mood and my planning mood. At the moment I am writing this I am in my thoughtful mood. When I am in my thoughtful mood I think out my maths and plan stories and poems. When my kitten is in her thoughtful mood she thinks shall I pounce or not, and shall I go to sleep or not. This sort of thing goes on in my own mind too. It is very hard for me to put my thoughts into words.

Sarah Gristwood, aged 7

stodgy: heavy and solid (like thick porridge)
loose-end: if someone is at a loose end, he doesn't know what to do to amuse himself
grumpy: bad-tempered
pounce: jump (to attack)

All about me

By me, myself, your's truly

I'm twelve years old. I'm large for my age and have big feet which I am self-conscious about. I look like both my mum & my dad but in different ways. I have fair hair and blue eyes like my dad, and a mouth & expression like my mum. My nose is like my mother's and deffinitly nothing like my father's ('thank goodness'). I am very like my mum in temperament, though I don't have her very hot temper.

I'm rather a tomboy but I'm not violent. I hate fighting & arguments. I hate being laughed at and some teasing hurts me more than I show. I tend to sulk when I am annoyed and I tend to be a bit over-sensitive. Friendship is important to me with people of all ages. My home is very important to me and I would hate to be sent to boarding school. On the whole I'm a fairly tidy person.

I am quite creative with my hands, I like making models, pendants and candles as well as other things. I like acting & music, I play the French horn & can play the trumpet. I am not a very keen reader because I like to be outside most of the time. I ride my bike a lot and have been youth hosteling with it. My father lives abroad and I enjoy travelling to see him. I enjoy my food (especially my French grandmothers as she is an excellent cook!) and I have a sweet tooth but I hate the dentist. I don't like my hair being brushed by someone else and I hate it long.

Finally the one thing I really find boring is homework as I would far rather be outside or making something.

(School homework by Ruth, aged 12)

your's truly: (should be written with no apostrophe) a humorous way of saying 'myself'
tomboy: a girl who likes boys' games
teasing: laughing at people
sulk: stay in a bad temper without talking
boarding school: a school in which the children live during term-time
pendant: piece of jewellery hung on a chain from the neck
youth hosteling: (correct spelling hostelling) touring, spending the nights in youth hostels
I have a sweet tooth: I like sweet things

The school that I'd like

[Some children's opinions of the British educational system.]

Stephen, 13

'Now, do you all understand?' asks the frowning old maths master impatiently. Silence! 'Right then, get on with pages seventy-two to seventy-six.' The heads bow down and pens begin to scratch. A few poor boys, still not understanding, sit waiting anxiously for the bell. Others glance at the clock every few minutes. The bell goes and the tension breaks; everyone hurriedly packs his books and heaves a sigh of relief. The master walks out and the next walks in. Another forty tedious minutes. . .

I go to a grammar school and this is a fairly accurate description of what a lot of the lessons are like. All this is wrong.

Angela, 13

Schools should be made better and made into a place *all* children like to go to and a place where you go because you want to go. Subjects should be made more exciting instead of sitting in a desk reading or half-listening to a teacher going on and on about a particular thing. I should like to be doing things, finding what I can do and what I can't do; not just talking about, e.g., a dairy farm but talking to the people who work there and trying to milk a cow by yourself.

Kari, 13

History and geography are dealt with adequately, but psychology and politics, drug-taking and smoking and love and death are not mentioned in the school syllabus at all.

Cosette, 17

Give us a more varied syllabus! Give us the chance to visit more frequently factories, to talk with miners, dustbin men, doctors, lawyers, jail-birds and addicts too. Give us the chance to visit remand homes. Prisons like Holloway, Pentonville, Parkhurst. We want to know more about life and a bit less about books.

Lyne, 15

The fault with a lot of schools today is that teachers are not prepared to listen. There is a teacher at our school who is very keen on discussions until somebody makes a point which she is unable to explain, and she gets angry and tells us to sit down. I think that's the attitude of most teachers today.

They don't mind discussing various topics as long as it ends up with them being able to prove a point to you and not the other way.

(Edward Blishen (ed.), *The School That I'd Like*)

heaves a sigh: breathes out loudly
tedious: boring
jail-birds: prisoners
addicts: people who are dependent on drugs
remand homes: homes for children who have broken the law

Energy

[From a tape-recording of a lesson in a junior school.]

Teacher	*Pupils*

1. Put your pens down; pencils down; fold your arms; look at the window; look at the ceiling; look at the floor; look at the door; look at me. Good. Now ... Before I came to school this morning, I had my breakfast. I had some cereal, and I had some toast, and I had an egg, and I had a cup of tea, and then I had a biscuit, and then I came to school. And you probably did the same sort of thing. You may have had a chuppati, or you may've had some chocolate, or you may've had some pop. I don't know what you have for breakfast: we have some weird and wonderful things. But you probably had some breakfast. And at dinnertime, in school, if you had the same dinner as me, you had fish, potatoes and cabbage, and then you had some lemon meringue and some custard, and, when you go home tonight, you'll probably have some more tea. Something else to eat. You'll fill yourself up. Perhaps with some more fish and chips. Or perhaps with just some meat and potatoes. Or perhaps with some cream cakes. And then before you go to bed, you might have something else to eat: hot drink and a sandwich and a biscuit perhaps. And then you'll climb into bed, and you'll go to sleep. Now tell me: why do you eat all that food? Can you tell me why do you eat all that food?
Yes.

2. To keep you strong.

Teacher	Pupils

Teacher

3. To keep you strong. Yes. To keep you strong. Why do you want to be strong?

5. To make muscles. Yes. Well what would you want to use – what would you want to do with your muscles?

7. You'd want to . . .

9. You'd want to use them. Well how do you use your muscles?

11. By working. Yes. And when you're working, what are you using apart from your muscles? What does that food give you? What does the food give you?

13. Not only strength; we have another word for it.
Yes.

15. Good girl. Yes. Energy. You can have a team point. That's a very good word. We use . . . we're using . . . energy. We're using . . . energy. When a car goes into the garage, what do you put in it?

17. You put petrol in. Why do you put petrol in?

19. To keep it going; so that it will go on the road. The car uses the petrol, but the petrol changes to something, in the same way that your food changes to something. What does the petrol change to?

23. You told me before.

26. Again.

28. Energy. Tell everybody.

30. Energy. Yes. When you put petrol in the car, you're putting another kind of energy in the car from the petrol. So we get energy from petrol and we get energy from food. Two kinds of energy.

Pupils

4. Sir, . . . muscles.

6. Sir, use them.
8. Use them.

10. By working.

12. Strength.

14. Energy.

16. Petrol.
18. To keep it going.

20. Smoke.
21. Water.
22. Fire.
24. Smoke.
25. *Inaudible*.
27. *Inaudible* (Energy).
29. Energy.

cereal: food made from corn (such as corn flakes)
chuppati: kind of Indian pancake
pop: (slang) bottled drink with gas in it
weird: strange
inaudible: impossible to hear

OXFORD HIGH SCHOOL

Name Kate Sumor   Summer Term   Age 13.4

Form Lower IV C   1975   Average Age of Form 13.3

SUBJECT	Term Mark	Exam Mark	REMARKS
Scripture	B+	68	Interesting work. HM.
English	B++	64	Kate's work shows intelligence but it could be much more clearly and carefully written. VJ.
History	B+	68	Promising work. HM.
Geography	B++	66	Kate has worked with interest & uses her own knowledge effectively. AC
Maths Div. 2	B	49 / 51	Kate is still rather disorganised in her work. She seems to quite enjoy her Mathematics but I think she will benefit from going a bit slower with division 3. G.P.S.
French Div. I	B+	68	Kate shows keen interest, & has vocabulary & style are improving, but she is still too apt to write without thinking, & thus her work is spoilt by careless mistakes. Aural it is still badly prepared.
German			
Greek			
Latin Div.	B-	75	It is a pity that she decided to work so late in the year as it has put her at a disadvantage, but she is beginning to catch up. LS
Chemistry			
Physics			
General Science or Biology	B	44	Kate works with intelligence, but must learn her facts more thoroughly, and express them more clearly. S.M.E.
Art	B	5	Kate works with interest but needs to extend her range of subject matter. She is gainirg control eff of different media.
Needlework	B++		Kate has tried very hard. She is now much better. Kw.
Music			Kate has had a very good year. JRn
Physical Education			Kate always tries hard when she does games. CB.

GENERAL REMARKS

Kate is trying to discipline herself to some extent, but I do not think she realises the value of slower, more careful work. She is most responsible and sensible in the form.

Late ....   Absent 5½   Head Mistress Elani Karg

Next Term begins on September 11th   Form Mistress DRogers

THIS REPORT SHOULD BE BROUGHT TO SCHOOL FOR ANY DISCUSSION ON THE PUPIL'S WORK

Good grief!: an exclamation (similar to *Oh dear!* or *Oh my God!*)

'On behalf of all your teachers, Ronald, I cannot express too deeply our sorrow that end of term brings us to the parting of the ways.'

the parting of the ways: the time when we have to say 'goodbye'

What did you learn in school today?

What did you learn in school today,
Dear little boy of mine?
What did you learn in school today,
Dear little boy of mine?
I learned that Washington never told a lie,
I learned that soldiers seldom die,
I learned that everybody's free,
That's what the teacher said to me,
And that's what I learned in school today,
That's what I learned in school.

What did you learn in school today,
Dear little boy of mine?
What did you learn in school today,
Dear little boy of mine?
I learned that policemen are my friends,
I learned that justice never ends,
I learned that murderers die for their crimes,
Even if we make a mistake sometimes,
And that's what I learned in school today,
That's what I learned in school.

What did you learn in school today,
Dear little boy of mine?
What did you learn in school today,
Dear little boy of mine?
I learned our government must be strong,
It's always right and never wrong,
Our leaders are the finest men,
And we elect them again and again,
And that's what I learned in school today,
That's what I learned in school.

What did you learn in school today,
Dear little boy of mine?
What did you learn in school today,
Dear little boy of mine?
I learned that war is not so bad,
I learned about the great ones we have had,
We fought in Germany and in France,
And someday I might get my chance,

And that's what I learned in school today,
That's what I learned in school.

Tom Paxton

Washington: George Washington

King Henry the eight fell in love lots of times and in the end they had to chop his head off because he was geting fat.

Sidney aged 7

Queen Victoria's breakfast

Queen Victoria enjoyed her breakfast, Never before or since has an egg been eaten in such state. It sat, this royal breakfast egg, in a gold eggcup which, in turn, stood on a gold plate. It was conveyed to the royal mouth by a gold spoon and behind the Queen's chair stood two Indian servants, resplendent in blue and gold uniforms. Queen Victoria also enjoyed her dinner which was, by our feeble modern standards, a gargantuan meal. But Queen Victoria at lunch – ah, that must have been a brave sight. Her lunches were the kind that have now vanished from the earth. Eight to ten courses with a water ice flavoured with rum served half-way through to rest the stomach. And the Indian servants ready with bowls of curry just in case someone could be persuaded to try some – which, in view of the size of the rest of the meal, seems unlikely.

(*Nova*)

in such state: with such ceremony
resplendent: looking splendid
gargantuan: enormous
a brave sight: a wonderful sight

The Irish famine

No event has had such a decisive effect in shaping the attitude of the Irish people towards the British. And although it occurred 120 years ago its effects are still apparent in Ireland today.

Looking back on the famine, the most remarkable fact was that it should ever have reached such proportions: although the potato crop failed there was plenty of food left in Ireland, and while thousands died some of it was being exported. Even if the local organizations for dealing with a crisis of such magnitude were completely inadequate, more positive and generous action by the British Government could have averted some of the worst effects. In the light of the large-scale Government relief projects undertaken today, the supreme irony of all was that the richest nation in Europe should have allowed one of the poorest to starve on its doorstep.

Yet the famine looked very different through nineteenth-century eyes. Then, the principles of *laissez-faire* were generally accepted – in fact, were regarded as almost sacred. It was thought that people should help themselves, and that the Government should not intervene. In the case of the Irish famine, it was argued, the Government had done all it could to help.

This argument may or may not be valid; but a little more humanity by the Government could have done no harm, and it seems strange that the reports of suffering that are so moving today could have failed to move the Government towards a greater use of its resources.

One million people died of starvation and disease; three-quarters of a million emigrated to America, there to become a despised and exploited class. Out of this disaster was forged a new and bitter feeling towards Britain. Daniel O'Connell, the 'Liberator', had insisted on non-violence in dealing with the British, and he had won almost universal support. But his era was over. The violent overthrow of the British rule was increasingly advocated, and hatred of Britain grew. Few Irish families had not been severely hit by the famine, and there were even fewer who did not lay the blame fairly and squarely at Britain's door.

(*New Knowledge*)

famine: extreme shortage of food
a crisis of such magnitude: such a great crisis
inadequate: not big or strong enough
averted: prevented
government relief projects: action by governments to help people who are suffering as a result of famines, floods, earthquakes, etc.
laissez-faire: principle that the government should not interfere in private economic activity
despised: looked down on   *era:* age, period
exploited: used for other people's profit   *advocated:* supported, recommended
forged: made

Why are so many hungry?

a Pelican Original

'If it takes you six hours to read this book, somewhere in the world 2,500 people will have died of starvation or of hunger-related illness by the time you finish.'

Why are so many hungry? Susan George affirms with conviction, and with solid evidence, that it is not because there are too many passengers on 'Spaceship Earth', not because of bad weather or changing climates, but because food is controlled by the rich. Only the poor go hungry.

The multinational agribusiness corporations, Western governments with their food 'aid' policies and supposedly neutral multilateral development organizations share responsibility for their fate. They all work in cooperation with local elites, themselves nurtured and protected by the powerful in the developed world. United States agripower paves the way, leads the pack and is gradually imposing its control over the whole planet.

Only those fortunate people who can become consumers will eat in the Brave New World being shaped by the well-fed. The standard liberal solutions to feeding the world – population control or the Green Revolution – are just what the hungry poor *don't* need. All they need is social change, otherwise known as justice. With that, they could, and would, resolve most of their problems themselves.

Cover design by John Carrod, photograph by Rod Shone

Economics
Science
Environment & Planning

United Kingdom £1.00
Canada $2.50

ISBN 0 14
02.2001 1

(Back cover of *How the Other Half Dies* by Susan George)

affirms: says emphatically   *conviction:* certainty
multinational corporations: companies which are based in several different countries
agribusiness: agricultural business
local elites: the people who have power and privileges in a particular country
nurtured: looked after   *agripower:* agricultural power
paves the way, leads the pack: is at the front
Brave New World: the title of a novel by Aldous Huxley, in which material conditions are very good but there is little real freedom
Green Revolution: a revolution in agriculture

Children's names for school food

Beefburgers: bath mats, door mats, shoe soles.
Cabbage: seaweed.
Chocolate mousse: Mersey mud.
Cornish pasties: dinosaur pies.
Currant pie: flies' cemetery.
Eggs, hard-boiled: hand-grenades.
Gravy: North Sea oil.
Lettuce: bats' wings, old men's faces.
Peas: bullets, stewed marbles.
Rice pudding with jam: road accident.
Salad cream: antiseptic spread.
Spaghetti: shoe-laces.

(*The Observer Magazine*)

Mersey: the river which flows into the sea near Liverpool
Cornish pasty: a kind of pie
hand-grenades: bombs thrown by hand
marbles: small glass balls used for children's games

PERFECT PAIRS
More unusual food combinations from our readers

● **MY** young grandson loves choco-late biscuits dipped in salad cream.
—M. E. Day: Cheltenham.

● **FOR** a sparkling new taste add a thin layer of orange, lemon or lime marmalade to the top of your piece of fish.—N. Ward: Weston-super-Mare.

● **SALT** and pepper sandwiches are amongst my husband's favourites.
—Mrs. L. Worth: Maxby.

● **MY** husband likes his strawberries to be liberally sprinkled with pepper.
—Mrs. G. Murdock: Sandy, Beds.

(*Woman*)

I always eat peas with honey:
I've done so all my life.
They do taste kind of funny,
But it keeps them on the knife.

(Anon.)

I don't like eating dead oranges

Emma aged 4

Veronica's Cream Cheese Custard Pie

Dough:

1/8 lb. butter (4 T.)
4 T. sugar
1 cup sifted flour
½ tsp. baking powder
Pinch of salt
1 beaten egg

Mix everything together well with hands. Fit into *deep* pie plate which has been greased. Put in refrigerator.

Filling:

½ lb. cream cheese
½ cup sugar
2 eggs–separated
1 tsp. vanilla extract
Juice of ½ lemon
1 T. flour
1½ cups milk

Soften cream cheese and mix with sugar; an egg beater or electric mixer speeds this up, but a wooden spoon is just as good. Add egg yolks, vanilla, lemon juice and flour; mix well. Add milk slowly; the consistency should be kept as smooth as possible. Beat egg whites stiff with a pinch of salt, then fold into batter. Pour into the dough-lined pan. Bake in 350° oven for 50 to 55 minutes, or until the center doesn't jiggle when you move it.

(V. Crum, *Eat It*)

dough: the mixture from which bread and pastry are made
lb.: pound (abbreviation of the Latin word *libra*); one pound is about 454 grams
T.: tablespoon (about 15 grams) *yolk:* the yellow part of an egg
sifted: with the lumps removed *batter:* the mixture that has just been made
tsp.: teaspoon (about 5 grams) *jiggle:* shake about

WE ACCEPT LV LUNCHEON VOUCHERS

HOT MEALS

```
SOUP OF THE DAY...................... 12
FISH   CHIPS............................ 42
ROAST CHICKEN   CHIPS PEAS.......... 60
ROAST LAMB   CHIPS PEAS............. 65
PORK CHOP  CHIPS PEAS................. 65
LAMB CHOPS   CHIPS  PEAS............. 60
LIVER  BACON   FRENCH FRIED........... 58
SIRLOIN STEAK  FRENCH FRIED TOMATOES..... 1.00

   special Texas grill, including steak. 1.10
..sausage  bacon  egg & chips........

STEAK PUDDING   CHIPS PEAS ....... 36
STEAK PIE · CHIPS  PEAS............. 36
SPAGHETTI BOLOGNESE.................... 42
CHICKEN, HAM & MUSHROOM PIE  CHIPS.....
RANCHBURGER  CHIPS................... 36
2 EGGS  BACON  CHIPS................. 45
SAUSAGE   EGG  CHIPS................ 34
EGG  BACON  CHIPS.................. 36
2 SAUSAGES  CHIPS.................. 34
1 EGG  CHIPS..25  2 EGGS CHIPS...... 33
EGG BACON.....27   BACON BEANS....... 27
KINGSIZE RANCHBURGER            25
EGG  OR  BEANS  ON  TOAST        15
```

TEA   COFFEE...   HOT SOUP 12   ★ ★

QUICK TAKE-AWAY SERVICE
PHONE YOUR ORDER

42

The menu of a first-class restaurant (the Elizabeth at Oxford)

[French – the language of gastronomy – is used for the names of the dishes in many better-class restaurants in Britain.]

Restaurant Elizabeth

MENU FOR

19th and 20th March

Minimum Charge – £3.25

Hors d'œuvre

Piperade	95p
A Basque dish of eggs with sweet pimento and tomato	
Avgolemono	85p
Chicken bouillon with beaten egg and lemon juice	
Ttoro	£1.25
A Basque fish soup served with Aioli	
Taramasalata	£1.25
A pâté of smoked fish	
Pâté de Foie de Volaille	£1.25
Escargots à la Bourguignonne	£1.35
Snails stuffed with butter, ½ doz.	
Mussels baked in butter	£1.25
Prawns with Rice and Aioli	£1.25
Shelled prawns with garlic mayonnaise	
Avocado Pear	£1.25
filled with prawns and Alabama sauce	
Avocado Pear	£1.25
Filled with soured cream and Danish caviar	
Quenelles de Saumon sauce Nantua	£2.25
Smoked Salmon	£2.75

Sweets

Lemon Sorbet	60p
Home made Rum ice cream	60p
Syllabub	60p
Chocolate Mousse	60p
Crème Brûlée	60p
Candied Chestnuts in Kirsch	60p
Cheese	60p

Main Dishes

Saumon en Papillot	£4.25
A steak of fresh salmon cooked in a paper bag with fish stock, white wine, herbs and butter	
Truite Alhambra	£3.25
Fresh river trout stuffed with a mousse of shellfish served with a wine and cream sauce	
Poulet au Porto	£3.05
Chicken marinated in Port wine and served with a Port wine sauce	
Suprème de Volaille au Vin Blanc	£3.05
Breast of Chicken in butter with cognac, white wine and cream	
Caneton à l'Orange	£3.45
Coq au Vin	£3.05
Escalopes de Veau Elizabeth	£3.05
Mousaka	£2.95
Lamb and beef baked with Aubergine, eggs and spices	
Carbonnade de Bœuf Flamande	£3.35
Beef steak cooked in Brown Ale	
Entrecôte Maison au Poivre Vert	£3.45
Entrecôte au Champignons	£3.45
Carré d'Agneau Dauphinois	
cooked specially to order for two people	
per portion	£3.45
Bœuf Stroganoff	£3.45
Filet de Bœuf Maison	£4.25
Chateaubriand	
cooked specially to order for two people	
per portion	£4.60

All these main dishes are served with either Saffron rice or Croquette and green salad.

The following vegetables are available

Chou-fleur au gratin	
Ratatouille	
Courgettes sautées au buerre	70p
Haricots Verts sautées au buerre	

Cover Charge	50p	**Cona Coffee**	50p

43

Leuntche

[An example of the strange things that can be found in 'conversation-guides' for foreigners.]

FRANCAIS-ANGLAIS

Déjeune-t-on (*ou* dîne-t-on) à la carte ou à prix fixe?	Is lunch (dinner) à la carte or at set price?	Iz leuntche (dinere) a la kahrte ohr ate séte praïce?
Quel est le prix du déjeuner?	How much do you charge for a lunch?	Haou meutche dou you tchahrdge fohr e leuntche?
A combien de plats a-t-on droit?	How many courses do you give?	Haou ménè kohrsece dou you guive?
Le vin est-il compris?	Is wine included?	Iz ouaïne innkloûdede?
Le café est-il compris?	Is coffee included?	Iz cofè innkloûdede?
Garçon, la carte.	Waiter, the bill of fare.	Ouaitere, dze bile ev faie-ere.
Quel est le plat du jour?	What is to day's dish?	Houate iz tou daice diche?

(*Manuel de Conversation avec Prononciation*, published in 1926)

à la carte: with each dish priced separately
bill of fare: old-fashioned expression for menu

"*Phrase-book*."

45

"Has phar la houdla seel vo plate?"

"Glhup hwow you shoul do da?"

Of what one sees in travelling, and of the events that may happen on the road.	*Was man auf der Reise sieht, und was sich unterwegs ereignen kann.*
Is this road safe? Are there any robbers on this road?	Ist die Strasse sicher? Giebt es keine Räuber auf dieser Strasse?
Postilion, stop; we wish to get down: a spoke of one of the wheels is broken; some of the harness is undone; a spring is also broken; one of the horses' shoes is come off.	Halt, Postillon; wir wollen aussteigen: es ist eine Speiche am Rade gebrochen; ein Zugriemen ist losgegangen; eine Feder ist zerbrochen; ein Hufeisen ist verloren.
The harness is mended. We can now get to the post-house without any danger.	Der Zugriemen ist wieder betestigt. Wir können nun ohne Getahr bis zur nächsten Station gelangen.
It begins to get dark. Do not leave us in the middle of the road during the night: whip your horses, get on, and take care not to overturn us.	Es beginnt dunkel zu werden; lasst uns nicht bis in die tiefe Nacht auf der Strasse liegen: peitscht eure Pferde und macht voran; werft uns auch nicht um.
You need not be afraid.	Seien Sie ohne Sorgen, meine Herren.
But the road is very steep and hilly; it is full of stones; there are precipices. Keep away from that ditch: it is full of mud.	Aber die Strasse ist sehr steil und bergig; sie ist voller Steine und hat Abgründe. Weg von dem Graben, er ist voll Schlamm.
For my part, I shall get out of the carriage; I wish to walk a little.	Ich für meinen Teil will aussteigen, ich will etwas zu Fusse gehen.
No, my friend; it is dark; you do not know the road; you might make a false step, fall, and meet with an accident; you might break an arm or a leg.	Nein, mein Freund; es ist dunkel; Sie kennen den Weg nicht, Sie möchten einen falschen Tritt thun, fallen und ein Unglück haben; Sie könnten einen Arm oder ein Bein brechen.
I shall ask these peasants, who are coming towards us, if the road by which they have come is bad.	Ich werde die Bauern fragen, welche da auf uns los kommen, ob der Weg, den sie zurückgelegt haben, schlecht ist.
It is unnecessary; here we are, thank God, at the inn safe and sound.	Das ist unnötig; da sind wir, Gott sei Dank, gesund und wohl beim Gasthofe angekommen.

(Extracts from Baedeker's *Traveller's Manual of Conversation*, published around 1900)

postilion: driver of the coach
spoke: long thin piece of wood or metal which connects the outside of a wheel to the centre
harness: the leather straps worn by a horse which is pulling a cart or coach
post-house: the place where travellers could rest and change horses
whip: hit
precipices: places where the ground falls away steeply

Misleading advice for foreigners

[The *New Statesman* magazine set a competition in which readers were asked to give misleading advice to tourists visiting England for the first time. These are some of the entries.]

Women are not allowed upstairs on buses; if you see a woman there, ask her politely to descend.

Visitors in London hotels are expected by the management to hang the bed-linen out of the windows to air.

Try the famous echo in the British Museum Reading Room.

On first entering an underground train, it is customary to shake hands with every passenger.

If you take a taxi, the driver will be only too willing to give your shoes a polish while waiting at the traffic-lights.

Never attempt to tip a taxi-driver.

Public conveniences are few; unfrequented streets where relief is permitted are marked 'P'.

Parking is permitted in the grounds of Buckingham Palace on payment of a small fee to the sentry.

Never pay the price demanded for a newspaper; good-natured haggling is customary.

public conveniences: public lavatories   *sentry:* soldier on guard
unfrequented: deserted   *haggling:* arguing about the price

(Advertisements in *Time Out*)

48

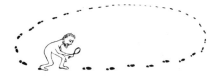

I'M IN SEARCH
OF MYSELF ──

HAVE YOU SEEN ME ANYWHERE?

Isle of Skye

Skye, the largest of the Inner Hebrides group of islands, 48 miles long and between 3 miles and 25 miles in breadth, is separated from the mainland of Scotland by the Sound of Sleat. Its bays and beaches, its rocks and its heather, its glorious Cuillin range of mountains combine to offer scenery of unsurpassed beauty and grandeur. Its historical and literary associations are of compelling interest while for the mountaineer, the walker, the fisherman, the artist or the photographer the island is a fascination itself and we hope that this all too brief publication will help you to find out more about Skye than would otherwise have been the case.

> Jerusalem, Athens and Rome
> I would see them before I die,
> But I'd rather not see any one of the three
> Than be exiled forever from Skye.
> (Alexander Nicholson)

Skye of all the Scottish Islands is the best known and the most loved. If it were not that the word has become almost meaningless today we would call it fabulous for that is what it is. Looked at on the map it seems to have newly broken away from the mainland and be about to fly away. The visitor will be told many different stories about place names but though some derive Skye from the Norse Ski meaning a cloud it is more likely to be from the Gaelic for winged.

(From a guidebook)

sound: narrow sea passage
heather: a mountain plant with purple or white flowers

exiled: sent away from one's own country
Norse: old Norwegian
Gaelic: the old language of Scotland

49

Making whisky: drying the malt

Green malt is not literally green – in fact it looks very like the original malted barley grains, a pale straw colour. It contains a considerable amount of moisture, and is transferred to the kiln for drying. It is the kiln that has the 'pagoda head' which proclaims the distillery on the landscape. The floor of the kiln is of perforated iron or wire mesh. Here the green malt is spread at a depth of between one and three feet (depending on the design of the kiln) and dried in the smoke arising from a peat fire some ten or fifteen feet below. The open ventilator at the top – which is the pagoda head – draws up the hot air from the fire through the green malt on the perforated floor. The peat is of the first importance as it gives its special flavour to the malt and eventually to the mature whisky. The smell of burning peat is an agreeable domestic smell when one experiences it in front of a peat fire in a Highland cottage. But if you put your face into the kiln when the peat smoke ('peat reek' as the Scots say) is billowing you will soon feel that enough is enough. The smoke stings the eyes and catches you in the throat, and though you may recognize that this is the flavour which will one day marvellously enrich the taste and bouquet of the matured whisky, you will probably be willing to wait for your next encounter until you meet it in the glass.

(David Daiches, *Scotch Whisky*)

malt: grains of barley (a kind of corn) that have started to grow
kiln: oven
distillery: place where whisky is made
perforated: with holes in
mesh: net
peat: a kind of fuel made from plant material dug out of bogs (very wet ground) and dried
ventilator: hole to let air in
mature: properly aged
billowing: blowing up in clouds
bouquet: smell (of a drink)

Make your own Scotch whisky

[This is an extract from an advertising pamphlet produced by the manufacturers of Teacher's Highland Cream whisky. The purpose is, of course, to show that it is much too difficult to make your own Scotch, and that the best thing is to buy 'Teacher's'.]

First pipe in a suitable supply of Scottish hill water, and add to this a goodly quantity of barley, allowing it to soak for 48 hours. Then strain off the water, and lay out the wet barley on a cool floor in a great heap. It will start to grow, and in doing so, will become hot.

So make a wooden spade, and every few hours turn it over, each time spreading it a little thinner on the floor to keep it cool. As barley grows 24 hours a day, you will have to set an alarm and get up regularly to carry out turning throughout the night.

This process takes only eleven days, and in your spare time you will have been able to construct a fire-place at the foot of a small brick tower which should have a wire gauze floor half-way up and a wooden imitation of a Chinese pagoda at the top with a hole in the roof.

Take your eleven-day-old barley, which by this

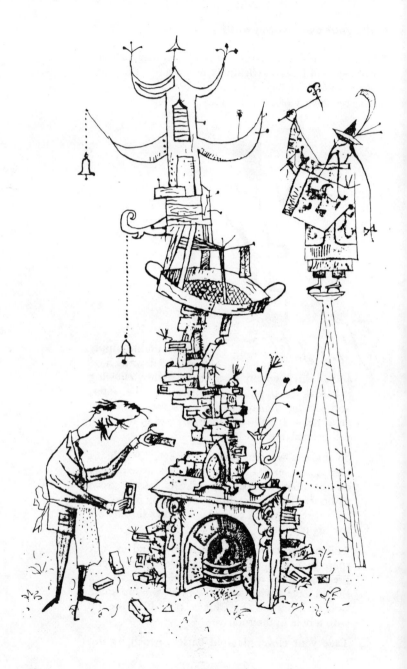

time will have grown a little shoot and a root, and spread it out carefully on the wire floor. What you have made is called malt. In the fire-place you must now build a huge fire of peat. This is a type of decomposed Scottish vegetation which is dug out of a bog the previous Spring, and carefully dried in what sunshine the following Scottish summer has to offer. This fuel is important as the peat smoke, which has a most nostalgic and haunting aroma, imparts some of this to the drying malt, and ultimately to the finished whisky, giving it flavour and character in much the same way as the smoke of wood chips gives us the delectable and appetising flavour of well-cured bacon or kippered herrings.

Every three hours dig over the drying malt, as otherwise it will burn on the lower side.

Unfortunately, as the fire cannot be put out, you will find the working conditions far from agreeable, and you will also notice that the smoke is not particularly nostalgic, but extremely haunting, and it will most probably haunt your clothes for the next four or five days.

After kippering the malt and yourself, the fire can be allowed to go out, and the malt will be found to be dry and hard. Remove the little root and shoot from each grain one by one, and give them to the birds. Then grind up the grains and add them to hot water, stirring vigorously.

wire gauze: wire net
shoot: the beginning of the stalk of the plant (the part above ground)
decomposed: rotten
haunting aroma: a smell that won't go away
imparts: passes, gives
cured: smoked
grind: crush to powder
vigorously: energetically

Definite, with a nervous elegance

[Experts on wine sometimes have a rather complicated way of expressing themselves. Here is a good example.]

Nineteen-seventy-five produced very good wines in apparently every region of Germany, and the 1975s demonstrate admirably why wines of the Rhine are great classics. Impressive but appealing, they exemplify the characteristics of their different regions in a way that is easy to understand. Here are only a few selected from recent tastings, ideal wines on which to form standards of fine hock. (The Mosels will be dealt with in a future article.)

Nahe wines can be soft and somewhat lacking in structure. But in 1975 they emerge definite, with a nervous elegance that is most pleasing. The Kreuznacher Brückes Riesling Kabinett of August Anheuser has a complex bouquet and great length and seems a bargain at £2.06. (From Dolamore, 16 Paddington Green, W2, and 15 Craven Road, W2, and their Oxford and Cambridge branches.) Sichel showed a wine new to me, beautifully constituted with charm as long as its name—Niederhäuser Harmennshöhle Riesling Spätlese from the Staatliche Weinbaudomäne at Niederhausen (£4.34 from Bow Wine Vaults, 10 Bow Churchyard, Cheapside, EC4). One step up in the scale is the Schloss Böckelheimer Kupfergrube Riesling Auslese, also from the Staatliche Weinbaudomäne, fruity but discreetly well-proportioned and a revelation to anyone previously supposing the Schloss Böckelheim wines to be somewhat obvious (£5.66 from O. W. Loeb, 15 Jermyn Street, SW1).

(Pamela Vandyke-Price, *The Times*)

hock: wines from the area of the river Rhine
Mosels, Nahe wines: wines grown near these two rivers

'It's a Naïve Domestic Burgundy Without Any Breeding. But I Think You'll be Amused by its Presumption'

breeding: good family or upbringing
presumption: attempt to appear better than one is

Notices in pubs

Everything I like is either immoral, illegal or fattening.

You don't have to be crazy to work here — but it helps.

WHY BE DIFFICULT, WHEN WITH A LITTLE EXTRA EFFORT YOU CAN BE ABSOLUTELY BLOODY IMPOSSIBLE

There are several reasons for drinking,
And one has just entered my head.
If a man cannot drink when he's living,
How the hell can he drink when he's dead?

I'll be sober in the morning, but you'll be crazy for the rest of your life   W.C. FIELDS

A MAN THAT LOVES WHISKY
AND HATES KIDS
CAN'T BE ALL BAD
W.C. FIELDS

I love mankind —
it's people I can't stand

The world needs more
people like US
and fewer like THEM.

The twelve bottles of whisky

I had twelve bottles of whisky in my cellar and my wife told me to empty the contents of every bottle down the sink – or else! So I said I would, and proceeded with the unpleasant task. I withdrew the cork from the first bottle and poured the contents down the sink, with the exception of one glass, which I drank. I extracted the cork from the second bottle and did likewise, with the exception of one glass, which I drank. I withdrew the cork from the third bottle and emptied the good old booze down the sink, except a glass which I drank. I pulled the cork from the fourth sink and poured the bottle down the glass, which I drank. I pulled the bottle from the cork of the next and drank one sink out of it and poured the rest down the glass. I pulled the sink out of the next glass and poured the cork down the bottle. I pulled the next cork out of my throat, poured the sink down the bottle and drank the glass, then I corked the sink in the glass, bottled the drink and drank the pour.

When I had emptied everything I steadied the house with one hand and counted the bottles and corks and glasses with the other, which were twenty-nine. To make sure I counted them again, when they came to seventy-four. And as the house came by, I counted them again, and finally I had all the bottles and corks and glasses counted, except one house and one cork, which I drank.

(Anonymous)

or else!: or something terrible would happen
booze: (slang) alcoholic drink

"No thanks — I don't drink."

When you are a baby your
mother feeds you from her
boZom but She can only do
milk.

Felicity aged 7

bozom: (correct spelling *bosom*) breasts

BEAR INN, Alfred Street   Ind Coope   44680

When you come here, make sure you are not wearing
a club tie because it might well end up in the
pub's collection. Around the walls you can see
what has happened to other people's neckwear -
there are about 300 specimens in glass cases. The
Bear dates from the Twelfth Century and remains
unspoilt. It is a cosy inn with a low ceiling and
three small bars. There is <u>real</u> Bitter on draught
and both hot meals and cold snacks are served.
During term-time, though, The Bear does tend to
get more than its fair share of 'chinless wonders'
from the aristocratic backwaters of Christ Church.

(From a guide to Oxford pubs)

Ind Coope: a firm of brewers (beer producers); they are the owners of this pub
cosy: comfortable
on draught: in barrels
chinless wonders: slang expression for upper-class people, many of whom are supposed
to have hardly any chin
Christ Church: a college in Oxford University; it has a high proportion of students
from upper-class families

Generally speaking, Whitbread landlords support the law. We only wish the reverse was always true.

Recently a lady who helps her husband run one of our pubs was sent flying across the room and on to the floor by a customer who objected to her asking him to drink up and leave.

This happened at 11.10 p.m., half an hour (and numerous requests) after the 10.40 p.m. "Last Orders" time.

When her husband came to her aid he was viciously attacked. His false teeth were broken, causing severe cuts to the inside of his mouth.

The barman was also beaten up.

The man was not drunk. He said in court that he had a couple of pints of lager earlier in the evening before coming to our pub. And two more pints while he was there.

The maximum penalty he could have received was five years in prison.

In fact, he got a three months sentence, suspended for one year and no fine.

Mercifully, this kind of maniacal violence is still comparatively rare in pubs. But there's no denying that there has been a steady increase in physical violence during recent years.

We don't claim to know why it's happening, or to have an answer to the problem.

But we do think the full penalties provided by the law should be used more than they are.

Certainly people who attack publicans should be dealt with at least as severely as people who attack other members of the public.

And this isn't the case at the moment.

(From an advertisement by Whitbread, the brewers, in *The Guardian*)

Whitbread: a firm of brewers
landlords: pub managers
'last orders': the last chance to buy a drink in a pub before closing time
penalty: legal punishment
suspended: the man would not have to go to prison if he kept out of trouble for a year
maniacal: violently mad
publicans: landlords of pubs

59

'I am standing under your foot.'

How to get rid of a wolf

This is a good technique to get rid of the beach-wolf who simply won't leave you alone to sunbathe in peace. If he becomes really tiresome, you could send him flying – literally – with a **Double foot lever throw.** Turn on your right side, and draw your legs up slightly towards you (this movement can be done on either side, of course). When the wolf is within range, hook your right foot quickly behind his left ankle, at the same time placing your left foot on his kneecap. Pulling sharply towards you with your right foot, kick his kneecap with everything you have in you, and you'll send him flat on his back. If he resists, you could break his kneecap, so don't use this one on somebody you hope to be dancing with later in the day.

(*Honor Blackman's Book of Self-Defence*)

wolf: a man who chases girls in an annoying way
tiresome: annoying
within range: close enough

Anger

I was angry and mad,
And it seemed that there was hot water inside me,
And as I got madder and madder,
The water got hotter and hotter all the time,
I was in a rage,
Then I began to see colours,
Like black and red,
Then as I got madder and madder,
My eyes began to pop out of my head,
They were popping up and down,
It was horrible,
And it would not stop,
I was steaming with anger,
Nobody could not stop me,
My mother could not stop me,
Then it was gone,
And I was all-right,
Horrible, black, madness.

Yvonne Lowe, aged 8

Two killed, 62 hurt in bomb attack on London Hilton

(Headline in *The Times*)

Americans and violence

[From an interview with a young American ex-soldier.]

Why do you think so many people are fascinated by violence?

'I think it's in the western world but especially in the States, because from the day I was born when I was watching television I was watching cats and mice fight in cartoons. And then I grew up a little older and not only did I see cats and mice fighting but I saw nice programmes with real people fighting on television. And then I just grew up a little more and I saw the real thing in the news and it didn't bother me a bit to see it because I'd been seeing it all my life. When I saw the news about Vietnam I saw Vietnamese, especially dead Vietnamese, they're not American, they don't bother you, you've seen it all your life. You saw dead Germans on television, you saw John Wayne kill millions of Indians, it doesn't bother you to see anybody who isn't a good American citizen dead. It's just imbedded in you from the day you're born. Violence is imbedded in people in the States. Especially if you get bored the easiest way out is to go and watch violence: watch the American soldiers beat the Japs.'

What is it like to be in the army?

'They teach you to respect discipline so they make you do whatever you don't like. Basically, they make you hurt yourself: they make you walk until you can't walk any more, they make you exercise until you're sore, they make you do training that makes you bleed, they make you crawl under bullets, they make you beat each other up, they make you watch films that instil nothing but violence and aggression – they take all this aggression and put it in you and then they turn you loose on something like a demonstration and then you take out all that aggression they've put in you and beat up the demonstrators. A few years ago they turned you loose in Vietnam and you took out all your aggression and shot women and children. That's what they do if you're in a low job like the infantry.'

John Wayne: American film actor who stars in (and directs) Western films
imbedded: fixed so that it can't be removed
Japs: (slang) Japanese
instil: teach
turn you loose on: send you to attack
infantry: foot soldiers

Amnesty International

Open your newspaper any day of the week, and you will find a report from somewhere in the world of someone being imprisoned, tortured or executed because his opinions or religion are unacceptable to his Government.

This quote, though of burning actuality, was written 15 years ago by Peter Benenson in that famous article 'The Forgotten Prisoner' in the British newspaper *The Observer*, which started the worldwide campaign for Amnesty International. This campaign, faintly recognized at first and taken up by but a few in those days of 1961, has since become a strong and dynamic international movement embracing membership and support in all five continents – a movement united to work on behalf of those imprisoned, tortured or executed because their opinions or religion are unacceptable to their government.

Amnesty International is unique in its structure and working methods. Close to 100,000 members throughout the world not only contribute financially for others to do the actual work, but they participate actively in campaigns to create public awareness and pressure on those governments which violate fundamental human rights. This large number of non-professionals has done more than any professional organization could ever have hoped to achieve within 15 years. They have made Amnesty International the largest international organization for human rights opposing, irrespective of political considerations, adamantly and unrelentingly, oppression and persecution for reasons of race, religion or conscientiously held belief.

(*Amnesty International Report 1975–76*)

actuality: importance now
campaign: large-scale movement
unique: unlike anything else
violate: attack, damage
adamantly: very firmly
unrelentingly: without weakening

> Your front page article about Africans being shot made me feel sick. Could not this kind of story be condensed and made more pleasant?

(From a letter in the *Daily Mirror*)

condensed: made shorter

Africa's plea

I am not you –
but you will not
give me a chance,
will not let me be *me*.

'If I were you' –
but you know
I am not you,
yet you will not
let me be *me*.

You meddle, interfere
in my affairs
as if they were yours
and you were me.

You are unfair, unwise,
foolish to think
that I can be you,
talk, act
and think like you.

God made *me*.
He made *you*.
For God's sake
Let me be *me*.

Roland Tombekai Dempster

meddle: the same as interfere

64

Immigrants in Blackburn

[From an interview with some apprentice mechanics in a pub.]

What about Blackburn as a place to live?

'It's all right. You're brought up to it, aren't you? You've lived here all your life, you get used to it.'

'Too many immigrants.'

'There ought to be some sort of control.'

'Stop 'em altogether.'

'If you let so many of them all live together, you'll get the same problem you've got in America.'

'We're not educating them to our culture though, are we? We're putting 'em in ghettoes.'

'You should let them come to go to universities, and then let them go back to their own country, educate their own people.'

'We asked them to come, though.'

'They're getting out of hand, living on the fat of the land.'

'There was a house, they were all sleeping in the rafters, hundreds of 'em.'

'First thing they do when they come in, most of 'em, is go down and see what they can claim, what they can get out of Social Security. That's the first thing they do. Some of them stop on the dole, claim for wives, it's a known fact that Pakistani families have at least five kids.'

(Jeremy Seabrook, *City Close-Up*)

Blackburn: an industrial town in the North of England
apprentice mechanics: boys who are learning to be mechanics by working with qualified workmen
ghetto: part of a town where immigrants are forced to live
out of hand: out of control
in the rafters: in the space under the roof
Social Security: the state organization for giving money to people who are unemployed
on the dole: receiving unemployment pay

An immigrant's point of view

[From an interview with Peter Lal, a thirty-five-year-old immigrant from East Africa.]

Among the immigrants, if somebody in the family is sick, or if he has any problem, then the rest of the members of the family share the responsibilities and the pain of that particular problem. Now, in this country, I have found that the English people, especially the young generation, don't respect the older people any more. When I go and look around the streets of this town, and when I see the hungry faces of the old people, I have found that they are very much crazy only for small conversation with people, because nobody talks to them. Nobody is ready to listen to them. Nobody helps them. The same type of life, family life, which is existing among the immigrants was existing among the people of this country. They had also a mutual understanding and respect for the family members and for the people who were living in the same street. . . . When the ladies in the old times were going out to work, other ladies looked after their family for them, looking after their cooking, looked after their clothes which they had put to dry outside their houses. Now this type of family life is what made the whole society happy. It's absolutely necessary. English people will automatically learn from the immigrants as they move in certain streets, and they will see immigrants living in the same way as their own parents used to live. They'll see that the children obey and respect their parents. These are some of the good aspects in the immigrants' way of life. The English people say, 'The immigrants must learn to be like us', and they do not always see that there are many things in the immigrants' lives that are better than the way the English people are living now. It is not only in their attitude towards the old people that the English can learn from the immigrants. With the children too. The immigrants' children do not say unkind and cruel things to their parents. But sometimes you hear Blackburn children say things to their mothers that you would not say to a dog. I see many social problems among the English that we do not have with the immigrants.

(Jeremy Seabrook, *City Close-Up*)

mutual: for each other

The holiday to end all holidays

[A West Indian immigrant's experience.]

I have been on holiday in England once. Since then I always take my
holidays in day outings to the seaside with my wife and little girl. We go off
to Brighton or Southend on the train, coming back the same night. I went
on holiday once, on a tour. With a friend and his wife, and me and my wife
(we didn't have children then) we set out in a car for a tour of the South East
– and since then I have never attempted to seek accommodation. We left
here at noon, intending to get bed and breakfast wherever we were that
night, and at nightfall we were in Bournemouth. We'd been around to
about ten places and were all told 'Sorry'. The car became a little low in
petrol so we went to a garage and the white manager there said: 'I'll take
you around; I'm sure I'll get you somewhere.' It was late September,
hardly the peak of the holiday season. We only wanted boarding-house
accommodation, not hotels. He took us to five places and came out with the
answer every time: 'Sorry, they won't take you.' Whether he knew the
managements or not I don't know. I think he did. When we asked him
whether they were full up, he'd reply: 'Sorry, I can't get you in.' Eventually
we decided to go into the back streets and my friend and I split up and
eventually found a place that had accommodation. We stood there for
fifteen minutes and eventually a chap came back and said: 'All right, we'll
have you.' We were well treated, the accommodation was good and we had
a nice breakfast. When they are full up you usually see the sign 'Full' but I
can't remember that we saw that once. I always understood accommodation
was reasonably easy to get in late September. Next day we made sure we
were near home at the end of the day and came back to our place. We never
even stopped to ask for any accommodation. I decided that was the end. It
might have been a bit defeatist but I decided that was the end. When my
little girl is a bit older I might change my mind and try it; all the kids look
forward to going on their holidays and I will have to fall in line. For myself
I'm not worried. I've always planned that if things get better I don't see why
my daughter can't spend her holidays in the West Indies. She wouldn't
encounter all the nonsense we encounter here.

(Derek Humphrey and Gus John, *Because They're Black*)

peak: busiest time
split up: separated
kids: (slang) children
fall in line: do the same as everybody else

A happy immigrant

'I'm happy here', says Lydia, 20, a secretary.
'I love it here. . . . When I came to England,
I was the only black kid in the road but I've
never had any trouble. . . . I used to mind
getting up every morning when it was cold,
thinking I could be back in the West Indies,
but now I'm quite happy. . . . You're quite free
here unless you get involved. I've never been in
trouble with the police.'

involved: politically active

*"Face facts, man—you're an under-
privileged black radical left-wing
unemployed person of no fixed address
with an Irish accent—of course you're
guilty!"*

ANYTHING TO DECLARE?

A customs officer suspicious about a lorry at Dover shouted: "Are you all right in there?" Back came the reply, "Yes" and 22 illegal Asian immigrants were discovered.

(*New Statesman*)

Two racist jokes

A man went into a pub with a big Alsatian dog. 'Good evening', he said. 'Do you serve Pakistanis?' 'Yes, sir, we do', replied the barman. 'Good, well fry him up a couple, will you, he's starving.'

How do you recognize an Irishman at an airport?
He's the one throwing bread to the aeroplanes.

starving: very hungry

Our first parents – Adam and Eve – were white. How then did the coloured races come into existence? This intriguing question baffles me.

(Letter in *Daily Mail*)

This . . . question baffles me: I can't understand it

Demonstration against race prejudice (TV report)

A demonstration against race prejudice drew
thousands of people to central London. It was
organized by the Labour Party and the Trades
Union Congress, under the banner 'United against
racialism'... The march was led by several
leading Labour Party and Trades Union officials.
Among them Mrs Barbara Castle, Mr Michael Foot,
and Mr Ron Hayward. It was a column that
stretched for over two miles and it took the
demonstrators nearly three hours to wend their
way from Speakers' Corner to Trafalgar Square.
There were representatives from more than twenty
major unions, as well as community workers and
various ethnic groups. By the time the march
reached Trafalgar Square an estimated 15,000
people had joined it. Mr Foot was one of the
more outspoken opponents of racialism:

'It breeds because of unemployment – we've got
to fight that too. It breeds because of
inflation – we've got to fight that too. It
breeds because of economic crisis, and people
come and say "Yes, this is the opportunity
to distract the attack on these evils and to
try and turn it into the evil of racialist
attack, as Hitler did in Germany before."'

```
Lord David Pitt, former chairman of the GLC, spoke
vehemently about the role of the black population:

'We have a right to demand privileges, we
have a right to demand rights, but we also
have a duty to accept our responsibilities,
and it is in that light that I address you
this afternoon.  It is only if both sides
will play their part fully that we will
achieve the society we want.'
```

(BBC1 television news 21 November 1976)

ethnic groups: groups of immigrants from particular parts of the world
breeds: grows, multiplies
GLC: Greater London Council (a local government body)
vehemently: violently, passionately
the role of the black population: their place and function in society

---

First day at school

But I was still shy and half paralysed when in the presence of a crowd, and my first day at the new school made me the laughing stock of the classroom. I was sent to the blackboard to write my name and address; I knew my name and address, knew how to write it, knew how to spell it; but standing at the blackboard with the eyes of the many girls and boys looking at my back made me freeze inside and I was unable to write a single letter.

'Write your name,' the teacher called to me.

I lifted the white chalk to the blackboard and, as I was about to write my mind went blank, empty; I could not remember my name, not even the first letter. Somebody giggled and I stiffened.

'Just forget us and write your name and address', the teacher coaxed.

An impulse to write would flash through me, but my hand would refuse to move. The children began to titter and I flushed hotly.

'Don't you know your name?' the teacher asked.

I looked at her and could not answer. The teacher rose and walked to my side, smiling at me to give me confidence. She placed her hand tenderly upon my shoulder.

'What's your name?' she asked.

'Richard.' I whispered.

'Richard what?'

'Richard Wright.'

'Spell it.'

I spelled my name in a wild rush of letters, trying desperately to redeem my paralysing shyness.

'Spell it slowly so I can hear it,' she directed me.

I did.

'Now can you write?'

'Yes, ma'am.'

'Then write it.'

Again I turned to the blackboard and lifted my hand to write, then I was blank and void within. I tried frantically to collect my senses but I could remember nothing. A sense of the girls and boys behind me filled me to the exclusion of everything. I realised how utterly I was failing and I grew weak and leaned my hot forehead against the cold blackboard. The room burst into a loud and prolonged laugh and my muscles froze.

'You may go to your seat,' the teacher said.

I sat and cursed myself. Why did I always appear so dumb when I was called to perform something in a crowd? I knew how to write as well as any pupil in the classroom, and no doubt I could read better than any of them, and I could talk fluently and expressively when I was sure of myself. Then why did strange faces make me freeze? I sat with my ears and neck burning, hearing the pupils whisper about me, hating myself, hating them.

(Richard Wright, *Black Boy*)

laughing stock: a person that everybody laughs at
giggled: laughed in a silly way
coaxed: encouraged me
titter: laugh quietly
flushed: went red in the face
redeem: compensate for
blank and void: empty
utterly: completely
dumb: stupid

Girl of 16 holds up class with shotgun

A girl aged 16 armed with a shotgun held up a class of children at a comprehensive school in Hampshire yesterday. A shot was fired into the ceiling as she was being overpowered by three police officers.

Police said that soon after school began at Amery Hill Secondary, Alton, the girl, armed with a single-barrelled shotgun belonging to her brother went into one of the classrooms and threatened a teacher and about 30 pupils.

" The police were called and despite all demands to persuade her she refused to hand over the gun. It became necessary to forcibly disarm her. As three police officers did so a shot went off and hit the ceiling ", police said.

A girl was taken to Alton police station for questioning.

(The Times)

shotgun: gun for shooting birds or small animals

'Girls, girls ! — A little less noise, please.'

She had two teenage children who, when younger, went through a phase of biting people. 'I bit them back and they stopped. My son, when about five, threw his dinner on the floor. I tipped a plate of custard over him. He hasn't thrown any food about since.'

(*Reveille*)

phase: period

Little Red Riding Hood

[Here are three unusual approaches to the well-known story of Red Riding Hood – the little girl who goes to visit her grandmother, and finds that she has been eaten by a wolf.]

The little girl and the wolf

One afternoon a big wolf waited in a dark forest for a little girl to come along carrying a basket of food to her grandmother. Finally a little girl did come along and she was carrying a basket of food. 'Are you carrying that basket to your grandmother?' asked the wolf. The little girl said yes, she was. So the wolf asked her where her grandmother lived and the little girl told him and he disappeared into the wood.

When the little girl opened the door of her grandmother's house she saw that there was somebody in bed with a nightcap and nightgown on. She had approached no nearer than twenty-five feet from the bed when she saw that it was not her grandmother but the wolf, for even in a nightcap a wolf does not look any more like your grandmother than the Metro-Goldwyn lion looks like Calvin Coolidge. So the little girl took an automatic out of her basket and shot the wolf dead.

Moral: It is not so easy to fool little girls nowadays as it used to be.

James Thurber

Calvin Coolidge: a President of the United States
automatic: a kind of pistol

74

The Bloodthirsty Story of
~~little~~ Big Blue riding hood

twice upon a time there
was a woolf who wanted
to eat up a big girl so he
Did...

he got intergestion
(searves him right)
but he Did
not live happily
ever after
he got Dwored
his kids got
much bigger
finally he
died and
rolled
away.
(what a drag)

[Written by a seven-year-old
child whose parents were
divorced]

twice upon a time: children's stories
often begin 'Once upon a time...'
intergestion: mis-spelling of
indigestion
what a drag: (slang) how boring

The little girl, the wolf, the grandmother and the psychologist

When Red Riding Hood visits her grandmother she finds that a wolf has usurped the grandmother's place. The protective, kindly figure has been replaced by a dangerous and destructive creature. It is this *exchange* of figures which makes the story particularly alarming. To encounter a wolf is frightening enough, but to find that one's loving grandmother has turned into this terrifying beast is to add to the situation that basic insecurity which springs from a sudden loss of trust in a person upon whom one relies. When an investigation was made into the effects of television programmes upon children, it was discovered that one of the things which most alarms the young is to find that an apparently 'good' and reliable parent is really a villain. So long as the good and the bad are separated, children can tolerate violence, death and other things which might be expected to disturb them. But to discover that the person one believed was on one's side is actually malign is to enter so unpredictable and unsafe a sphere of experience that children become alarmed; just as an adult might if he discovered that the injections which his doctor was giving him were poisonous rather than therapeutic.

To treat the wolf and the grandmother as opposite facets of the same person may appear nonsensical to some readers. Red Riding Hood does not realize, any more than any other small child can be expected to recognize, that grandmotherly solicitude and kindness which cherish and support the dependent young can, if overdone, turn into possessiveness and overprotection of a kind which prevents the child from developing into a separate person, and therefore threaten to swallow it, as the wolf actually does in the original version of the story. Yet protection and restriction are linked together inextricably; and the very person upon whom the child depends for its safety can easily become a tyrant if the child fails, or is not allowed, to escape from the maternal toils.

(Anthony Storr, *Human Aggression*)

usurped: taken over illegally
malign: bad, evil
therapeutic: effective in curing disease
facets: sides, aspects of a personality
solicitude: care
cherish: look after
overdone: exaggerated
swallow: eat up
linked together inextricably: inseparably connected
the maternal toils: dependence on the mother

WATCH THIS MAN

HE'S GOING INTO BATTLE

...and you can march right beside him by getting COMMANDO War Stories ... All the thrills of the war on Land, at Sea, and in the Air ... the blaze of action told in brilliant pictures ...

Remember the password—

Commando

War Stories in Pictures
8p each

(Advertisement in children's 'comic')

ALL THE RAW EXCITEMENT OF DEADLY CONFLICT!

12 picture titles every month in
WAR PICTURE LIBRARY

(Advertisement in children's 'comic')

conflict: fighting, battle

What's the matter up there?

'What's the matter up there?'
'Playing soldiers.'
'But soldiers don't make that kind of noise.'
'We're playing the kind of soldier that makes that kind of noise.'

Carl Sandburg

Children: violence, creativity and reading

[The author is writing about her experiences as a primary school teacher in New Zealand.]

I see the mind of a five-year-old as a volcano with two vents: destructiveness and creativeness. And I see to the extent that we widen the creative channel, we atrophy the destructive one. . . . I can't dissociate the activity in an infant room from peace and war. So often I have seen the destructive vent, beneath an onslaught of creativity, dry up under my eyes. Especially with

78

the warlike Maori five-year-olds who pass through my hands in hundreds, arriving with no other thought in their heads other than to take, break, fight and be first. With no opportunity for creativity they may well develop, as they did in the past, with fighting as their ideal of life. Yet all this can be expelled through the creative vent, and the more violent the boy the more I see that he creates, and when he kicks the others with his big boots, treads on fingers on the mat, hits another over the head with a piece of wood or throws a stone, I put clay in his hands, or chalk. He can create bombs if he likes or draw my house in flames, but it is the creative vent that is widening all the time and the destructive one atrophying, however much it may look to the contrary. And anyway I have always been more afraid of the weapon unspoken than of the one on the blackboard.

. . . The reading is very much on my mind. All my other interests in the writing world are put aside until I satisfy myself on this matter. I am continuing experiments at school on the words of most vital meaning to a child to begin with. These words seem to be sorting themselves out with alarming clarity around the two main instincts, fear and sex.

I began to suspect this when I tried the word 'kiss'. The children, five-year-old Maoris, discussed it excitedly. They returned to the book to find the place once more and the next morning ran in early to tell us that they could still spell 'kiss'. I took the hint and looked for a word to represent the first and strongest instinct, fear. But the only one I had was 'frightened', which did not recommend itself as a first word on account of its length. Although I knew that it has always been an easy word to teach, and one that I have always used extensively. However, I tried it, and it won, even against 'kiss', which is according to the importance of the two instincts. It was learnt immediately by the new entrants, and another thing occurred that I had not noticed before. An intelligent, new Maori, just five, repeated the word 'frightened' over and over again to himself.

. . . Here is the impromptu reading card on which one of my backward Maori five-year-olds at last learned to read. He read it on sight, and by the lighting up of his face, he *understood*.

Daddy   Mummy   Ihaka   hit   cried   kiss

Daddy hit Ihaka.   Ihaka cried.   Mummy kissed Ihaka.

Daddy hit Ihaka.   Ihaka cried.   Kiss Ihaka Mummy.

Questioned on it he understood it. He has stalled for about six weeks on 'come', 'and', 'look'.

. . . It is an opportune moment to observe the emotional distance of these private key vocabularies from the opening words of the 'Janet and John' book:

Janet   John   come   look   and   see   the   boats   little   dog   run
here   down   up.

. . . Sometimes I relax the children with eyes closed to dream. When they awake I hear these dreams. The violence of those has to be heard to be believed. A lot of it is violence against me – which they tell me cheerfully enough. I come out very badly. My house has been burnt down, bombs fall on me, I'm shot with all makes of guns and handed over to the gorilla. Presumably it's the authority and discipline which I represent.

The distance between the content of their minds, however, and the content of our reading books is nothing less than frightening. I can't believe that Janet and John never fall down and scratch a knee and run crying to Mummy. I don't know why their mother never kisses them or calls them 'darling'. Doesn't John ever disobey? Has the American child no fears? Does it never rain or blow in America? Why is it always fine in primer books? If these questions are naive it must be because of the five-year-old company I keep. Heaven knows we have enough lively incident in our Maori infant rooms. The fights, the loveships, and the uppercuts from the newcomers. I see the respectable happy reading book placed like a lid upon all this – ignoring, hiding and suppressing it.

(Sylvia Ashton Warner, *Teacher*)

vents: openings
atrophy: make smaller and weaker
dissociate: separate
infant room: classroom for small children
onslaught: attack
Maori: the Maoris were the original inhabitants of New Zealand
clay: kind of earth used for making statues, cups, etc.
vital: deeply important
hint: suggestion
entrants: children starting school
impromptu: made without planning
backward: behind the others in school work
on sight: as soon as he saw it
stalled: been stuck
an opportune moment: a good moment
'Janet and John': characters (brother and sister) in a series of children's reading books produced in the USA
disobey: do what he is told not to
primer books: first reading books
loveships: a word invented by the author (compare *friendships*)
uppercut: a punch used in boxing

Peter and Jane

[Extract from an English children's reading book.]

Peter is at work with his daddy. He likes to work with his daddy.

"Go away," he says to Pat, "go away. Be off. Be off, I want to work."

Daddy says, "Put the things down there, and then help me make a fire."

Peter puts his things down. "Good," he says, "I want to make a fire."

Peter helps his Daddy to make a big fire.

"I like this work," says Peter.

"It is like play," says Jane. "Put some things on the fire, Daddy wants a big fire."

"Yes," says Daddy, "make a big fire. Keep the dog away. Keep Pat away."

"Come here, Pat," says Jane, "come to me. Be a good dog and keep away."

You can see Daddy at his big fire.

(Ladybird Books Ltd, *Things We Do*)

Pat: the dog
be off: go away

Susan and John

[A child's satire on the 'Peter and Jane' books.]

Fire.

Susan and John ~~are~~ are in the garden. Rover is in the garden too. There is a big fire in the garden; a big, hot fire. Daddy is also in the garden. Susan and John and Rover are smiling. Where is daddy? Yes where is daddy? Is daddy playing on the big, hot fire?

Shopping with mummy

John and Susan and mummy
are ~~they~~ going shopping.
Susan and John and mummy
are buying some eggs. Now
they are buying some cheese.
Now they are coming out
of the shop.
"Be very careful, now, be
careful when you cross
the road." Says mummy.
Oh dear, a big car has
hit mummy — a big, big,
car. Oh dear. Is daddy
driving the big car?

Kate, aged 9.

Rover: a dog's name

Jim

WHO RAN AWAY FROM HIS NURSE, AND
WAS EATEN BY A LION

There was a Boy whose name was Jim;
His Friends were very good to him.
They gave him Tea, and Cakes, and Jam,
And slices of delicious Ham,
And Chocolate with pink inside,
And little Tricycles to ride,
And
   read him Stories through and through,
And even took him to the Zoo –
But there it was the dreadful Fate
Befell him, which I now relate.

You know – at least you *ought* to know,
For I have often told you so –
That Children never are allowed
To leave their Nurses in a Crowd;

Now this was Jim's especial Foible,
He ran away when he was able,
And on this inauspicious day
He slipped his hand and ran away!
He hadn't gone a yard when –

Bang!

With open Jaws, a Lion sprang,
And hungrily began to eat
The Boy: beginning at his feet.

(Extract from Hilaire Belloc, *Cautionary Tales for Children*)

nurse: servant employed to look after children
the dreadful fate befell him: the terrible thing happened to him
relate: tell
foible: weakness of character
inauspicious: unlucky

Counting-out rhymes

A little green snake ate some cake
And then he had a belly-ache.
Butter, sugar, coffee, tea,
You are not he!

Ip, dip, sky blue
Who's it? Not you!

counting-out rhymes: rhymes used by children to decide who will play a particular part
in a game (members of the group are 'counted out' until only one is left)
belly-ache: stomach-ache
ip, dip: nonsense words

Skipping (rope-jumping) rhymes

I am a brownie dressed in brown
How many miles do I walk to town?
One, two, three . . . [until a mistake is made].
I am a girl guide dressed in blue
These are the things I have to do:
Salute to the King
Curtsey to the Queen
Show my knickers to the football team.

I like coffee, I like tea,
I want [name] in with me.
I don't like coffee, I don't like tea,
I don't want [name] in with me.

brownie, girl guide: members of girls' organizations (the girl guides are the girls'
equivalent of the boy scouts; younger girls can become brownies)
salute: raise the hand to the hat (like a soldier greeting an officer)
curtsey: bend the knee as a sign of respect
knickers: girls' underpants

The function of children's rhymes

... through these quaint ready-made formulas the ridiculousness of life is underlined, the absurdity of the adult world and their teachers proclaimed, danger and death mocked, and the curiosity of language itself is savoured.

Iona and Peter Opie, *The Lore and Language of Schoolchildren*

quaint: strange and amusing
proclaimed: announced
mocked: laughed at
savoured: enjoyed
lore: traditional knowledge

Matthew, Mark, Luke and John
Went to bed with their trousers on.
Mark cried out in the middle of the night
'Oh, my trousers are too tight.'

(Children's rhyme)

One fine day in the middle of the night,
Two dead men got up to fight.
Back to back they faced each other,
Drew their swords and shot each other.
A paralysed donkey passing by
Kicked a blind man in the eye,
Knocked him through a nine-inch wall
Into a dry ditch and drowned them all.

(Children's rhyme)

ditch: water-channel at the side of a road

Tonight at noon

Tonight at noon
Supermarkets will advertise 3d EXTRA on everything
Tonight at noon
Children from happy families will be sent to live in a home
Elephants will tell each other human jokes
America will declare peace on Russia
World War I generals will sell poppies in the streets on November 11th

The first daffodils of autumn will appear
When the leaves fall upwards to the trees

Tonight at noon
Pigeons will hunt cats through city backyards
Hitler will tell us to fight on the beaches and on the landing fields
A tunnel full of water will be built under Liverpool
Pigs will be sighted flying in formation over Woolton
and Nelson will not only get his eye back but his arm as well
White Americans will demonstrate for equal rights
in front of the Black House
and the Monster has just created Dr Frankenstein

Girls in bikinis are moonbathing
Folksongs are being sung by real folk
Artgalleries are closed to people over 21
Poets get their poems in the Top 20
Politicians are elected to insane asylums
There's jobs for everyone and nobody wants them

In back alleys everywhere teenage lovers are kissing
in broad daylight
In forgotten graveyards everywhere the dead will quietly
bury the living
and
You will tell me you love me
Tonight at noon

Adrian Henri

3d: threepence (before the change to decimal currency)
November 11th: Armistice Day (the anniversary of the end of the First World War);
poppies are sold in the streets, and the money goes to old soldiers and their dependants
to fight on the beaches . . .: a quotation from a war speech by Churchill
Top 20: list of best-selling pop records
back alleys: small streets behind the houses

I'll tell my ma

Briskly

I'll tell my ma when I go home,
The boys won't leave the girls alone
They pulled my hair, they stole my comb,
But that's all right till I go home.
She is handsome, she is pretty,
She is the belle of Belfast city.
She is courting, one, two, three,
Please will you tell me who is he?

Albert Mooney says he loves her,
All the boys are fighting for her.
They rap at the door, they ring at the bell,
Say 'Oh my true love, are you well?'
Out she comes as white as snow,
Rings on her fingers, bells on her toes.
Old Johnny Morey says she'll die
If she doesn't get the fellow with the roving eye.

Let the wind and the rain and the hail blow high,
And the snow come travelling from the sky.
She's as nice as apple pie,
And she'll get her own lad by and by.
When she gets a lad of her own
She won't tell her ma when she comes home.
Let them all come as they will,
It's Albert Mooney she loves still.

(Irish children's street song)

belle: most beautiful girl
she is courting: she's got a boyfriend
the fellow with the roving eye: the man who likes to have a lot of girlfriends
(roving = wandering)
lad: boy
by and by: sooner or later

Warning to children

Children, if you dare to think
Of the greatness, rareness, muchness,
Fewness of this precious only
Endless world in which you say
You live, you think of things like this:
Blocks of slate enclosing dappled
Red and green, enclosing tawny
Yellow nets, enclosing white
And black acres of dominoes,
Where a neat brown paper parcel
Tempts you to untie the string.
In the parcel a small island,
On the island a large tree,
On the tree a husky fruit.
Strip the husk and pare the rind off:
In the kernel you will see
Blocks of slate enclosed by dappled
Red and green, enclosed by tawny
Yellow nets, enclosed by white
And black acres of dominoes,
Where the same brown paper parcel –
Children, leave the string alone!
For who dares undo the parcel
Finds himself at once inside it,
On the island, in the fruit,
Blocks of slate about his head,
Finds himself enclosed by dappled
Green and red, enclosed by yellow
Tawny nets, enclosed by black
And white acres of dominoes,
With the same brown paper parcel
Still unopened on his knee.
And, if he then should dare to think
Of the fewness, muchness, rareness,
Greatness of this endless only
Precious world in which he says
He lives – he then unties the string.

Robert Graves

slate: a kind of blue-grey stone
dappled: with patches of different colours

tawny: yellowish brown
dominoes: flat pieces of wood, marked with spots, used in a game
husk: dry cover of a fruit or grain
pare the rind off: cut off the skin
kernel: inside of a seed or nut

Children's jokes

'What's yellow and dangerous?'
   'A canary with a machine gun.'

'What's black and white and black and white and black and white?'
   'A nun rolling downhill.'

'How do you know you've got elephants in the fridge?'
   'Footprints in the butter.'

'Why do elephants paint their toenails red?'
   'So that they can hide in the cherry-trees.'

'How do you get four elephants into a Mini?'
   'Two in the front and two in the back.'

'How do you get four giraffes into a Mini?'
   'You can't – it's full up with elephants.'

'What is an octopus?'
   'An eight-sided cat.'

'What is a fjord?'
   'A Norwegian car.'

" You're improving. You used to shoot your own foot."

-ACKEN·

93

King of the jungle

The lion was feeling pretty good as he prowled through the jungle. Seeing a tiger, the lion stopped it.

'Who is the King of the jungle?' the lion demanded.

'You, O lion, are the King of the jungle', replied the tiger.

Satisfied, the lion strolled on, until he came across a large, ferocious-looking leopard.

'Who is the King of the jungle?' asked the lion, and the leopard bowed in awe. 'You, mighty lion, you are the King of the jungle', it said humbly and walked off.

Feeling on top of the world, the lion proudly marched up to a huge elephant and asked the same question. 'Who is the King of the jungle?'

Without answering, the elephant picked up the lion, swirled him round in the air, smashed him to the ground and jumped on him.

'Look,' said the lion, 'there's no need to get mad just because you didn't know the answer.'

prowl: word used to describe the way hunting animals move, especially when they are looking for food
ferocious: fierce
awe: deep respect
mighty: powerful and strong

Softly

Strong and long
The tiger crouches down
Orange and black in
the green grass
Careful little fawn how
you pass.

Peter Sandell, aged 8

fawn: baby deer

"Get me the Zoo, please, Miss Winterton."

Self-pity

I never saw a wild thing
sorry for itself.
A small bird will drop frozen dead from a bough
without ever having felt sorry for itself.

D. H. Lawrence

The beasts

I think I could turn and live with animals, they are so
     placid and self-contain'd;
I stand and look at them long and long.
They do not sweat and whine about their condition;
They do not lie awake in the dark and weep for their sins;
They do not make me sick discussing their duty to God;
Not one is dissatisfied – not one is demented with the
     mania of owning things;
Not one kneels to another, nor to his kind that lived
     thousands of years ago;
Not one is respectable or industrious over the whole earth.

Walt Whitman

placid: peaceful
self-contained: independent
whine: complain
demented: mad
mania: madness
industrious: hard-working

Meditatio

When I carefully consider the curious habits of dogs,
I am compelled to conclude that man is the superior animal.
When I consider the curious habits of man,
I confess, my friend, I am puzzled.

Ezra Pound

compelled to conclude: forced to decide

Dog Dracula

[This is an extract from a real conversation. Ann and Johnny, who live in Scotland, were on a visit to Oxford, together with their son (Philip) and their dog (Bossy); they were staying with Ann's mother (Ma). On the evening the conversation took place they had all gone to have a drink with Ma's daughter-in-law (Hazel-Ann), leaving the dog at Ma's house. The conversation was recorded by Philip, unknown to the others.]

ANN: I wake up about 10.30 or something and feel as if it's, you know, 7.30 or 8 in the morning.

JOHNNY: Change of air.

MA: It definitely is because I know what it did to me, and I was absolutely exhausted for the first fortnight when I came down here from Edinburgh. Then I gradually started working back, but – it *is* the change of air.

JOHNNY: Change of air.

MA: You did know we've got the dog too, did you?

HAZEL-ANN: Where is it?

MA: Well, it's not with us.

ANN: We've left him in Ma's with a pair of somebody's socks kicking around so he knows we're coming back.

MA: He goes – he's – you know the garden I've worked so hard on.

HAZEL-ANN: Well, all right, Ma, I –

MA: I don't in the least mind him scratching. But he's got a tree.

ANN: He loves that little tree in the corner.

MA: It's his great big back feet. Because I've made a little garden round it with four little pieces of dianthus that are growing very nicely.

HAZEL-ANN: They were. (*Laughter*)

MA: And he goes out and cocks his leg, well, that's fine, then he turns round with his bloody great big back feet, he scratches everything, my dianthus go flying in the air like that (*laughter*) and there's no garden any more.

ANN: Ma put one in a pot last night, so the dog knocked the pot over.

MA: Yes, I – 'Put it in a pot', she said. So he went out, and I put it in a pot and put it out at the side of the wall away from the garden; he went straight over, knocked the thing over, and God knows what he was going to do with it if I hadn't rescued it. It was his. He's a lovely dog though.

HAZEL-ANN: You know, but your – cat, your kitten, you know what he likes – more than anything else? And so do two of the others. Kleenex. You remember that Big Ben used to pinch socks?

MA: Yes, he did, run off with them, run away with them.

HAZEL-ANN: He stripped Katie of her nightie one day. (*Laughter*).

MA: He used to go – actually, you know, he did, he used to take it off.

HAZEL-ANN: He really did, and he – he – he took it and it – it w–went, you know, he – (*laughter*).

MA: He was running off with Kate's nightie. He always did this, but he loved to pinch socks.

ANN: Bossy doesn't steal as such, but I was telling Ma – eh – if I've got sweets in the message bag he'll go and take them.

HAZEL-ANN: What's a message bag?

MA & ANN: Shopping bag.

ANN: Shopping bag.

MA: They go messages, they don't go shopping. (*Laughter.*)

ANN: He'll always drop something in in its place. If he's going to take sweets he'll drop you a chewed up bit of paper in – it's 'fair exchange is no robbery'. And one day he had a whole packet of cinnamon balls – well, he didn't like them but he kept trying the next one to see if it was better than the one before (*laughter*) and he had them bitten in half all over the place when I came in from work. Couldn't see the place for cinnamon balls.

PHILIP: Tell them about your false teeth.

ANN: Oh, he did, yes, he took my bottom with four – four teeth on it – the bottom plate that I didn't always wear you see, so it was in the bag and Bossy –

PHILIP: Handbag.

ANN: – had them in his mouth.

HAZEL-ANN: Oh, no !

ANN: It was like a – a dog Dracula. (*Laughter.*)

working back: gradually getting back to where I was before
kicking around: lying around
dianthus: a plant
cocks his leg: lifts his leg up
Big Ben: Hazel-Ann's daughter's cat
pinch: (slang) steal
Katie: Hazel-Ann's daughter
nightie: night-dress
they go messages: Scottish people use the expression 'to go messages' instead of 'to go shopping'
cinnamon balls: a kind of sweet

THE DRAUGHT DOG

draught dog: dog used for pulling loads

I think rabbits make very good mothers

Sara aged 6

My dog wants to give all dogs he
meets babies. Hes a terrible responsiblity

Albert aged 7

I had a baby budgie called Tabatha
but she died before she knew what
she was.

Ruth aged 8

(Collected by Nanette Newman)

99

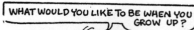

Thelwell

Age limits

age you have a right to

5 Go to school

7 Withdraw money from a post office savings account

10 Be convicted of a criminal offence provided prosecution can prove you knew what you were doing

13 Buy fireworks
Be employed for certain hours a week
Buy a pet animal
Be fingerprinted if in custody charged with an offence

14 Be convicted if you are male of a sexual or unnatural offence (also before this age in certain circumstances)
Own an air rifle
Take part in a public performance without a licence
Be held fully responsible for a crime
Pawn an article at a pawn shop
Play cribbage or dominoes in a room in a pub which is not a bar

15 Possess an assembled shot-gun if under the supervision of someone over twenty-one

16 Invest in Premium Bonds
Sell scrap metal
Join a trade union
Leave school
Choose your own doctor
Apply for social security benefit
Work full time
Age of consent for sexual intercourse (girls)
Leave home, with parents' consent

16 Enter, or live in, a brothel
Marry, with parents' consent
Hold a licence to drive certain tractors, ride a motor-
cycle and invalid carriage
Enter the bar of a pub but not buy a drink unless you
are also buying a meal in which case you can order
beer and wine

17 Hold a licence to drive any vehicle except certain heavy
vehicles
Enter a betting shop
Buy or hire firearms and hold a licence to possess a
firearm
Apply for a private pilot's licence
Engage in street trading

18 Age of majority
Leave home
Marry
Vote
Bring and defend accusations in court
Act as executor or administrator of a deceased person's
estate
Make a will
Change your name
Apply for a passport on your own responsibility
Buy and sell goods
Enter into hire purchase agreements
Apply for a mortgage
Be a full legal owner of house and land
Sue and be sued in the courts
Go abroad for the purpose of singing, playing,
performing or being part of an exhibition without a
licence
Buy drinks in the bar of a pub

18 Pay adult contributions to National Insurance schemes
Sit on a jury
Do almost anything an adult can do except –

21 Be a candidate in a parliamentary or local election
Hold a licence to drive any mechanically propelled
vehicle
Hold a licence to sell intoxicating liquor

(Nan Berger, *Rights*)

in custody: held by the police
charged with an offence: accused of breaking the law
pawn shop: place where you can borrow money if you leave a valuable object as
security
cribbage: a card game
Premium Bond: government loan certificate which gives the holder a chance to win a
prize
scrap metal: pieces of old metal
social security benefit: money paid by the government to unemployed people
brothel: house where prostitutes work
deceased: dead
mortgage: loan used to buy a house
sue: make a legal claim against somebody
jury: the twelve people who have to decide whether an accused person is guilty, in
certain court cases
intoxicating liquor: alcoholic drinks

A room of one's own

[From a tape-recorded conversation between five sixteen-year-old girls during an English lesson. A, B, C, D and E stand for the names of the speakers; words in brackets are interruptions.]

A Have you ever . . . you know . . . sort of . . . Mum's said to you, like, Could you help me clear up? So you say, Yes, O.K., and you put your brother's or sister's things away, and then they come up and they say, Where's so and so? (Yeah . . . Yes) But then you think to yourself, Well, it's annoying to have . . . to have . . . to leave somebody's coat or something in the middle of the room . . . (Yes . . . Yes, I know . . .) Do you know what I mean?

B And when they do complain, you feel as if you haven't done your job, but then you say, Well, I did pack it away, didn't I? . . . You know . . . what are they complaining about?

D It's annoying as well. . . .

E I do the same . . . I mean if I find anything lying around . . . if it's no good I just throw it away. . . .

A It might mean a lot. . . .

D I think in my family . . . I think my mother is the most considerate . . . she'd ask rather than my father . . . my father wouldn't.

A Well, I'm lucky . . . I've got a room of my own . . . so. . . .

D I'd like a room of my own, but then again, you don't keep everything in your room, do you? My dad or mother goes in there and finds anything that she doesn't think is necessary . . . my mother would ask me first, but my dad. . . .

B Well, frankly, my mother wouldn't touch anything in my room, you know . . . she just doesn't. She feels I've put it there for some purpose . . . but again, if I go into her bedroom . . . (Yeah . . . That annoys me. . . .) But say if I have a day off from school . . . or when . . . or we've got some sort of holiday and I see things around and I say, well, you know, I'll give the place a good old clean, at least it'll help . . . and I put things neatly, it's all tidy . . . I wouldn't throw anything out, because I'm not sure whether she wants it or not . . . and then she comes home, she says, Where's this? where's that? . . . I feel awful. . . .

D And you feel that . . . um . . . she doesn't appreciate. . . .

B . . . appreciate, you know . . . I even the other day moved her bedroom . . . er . . . (Furniture) . . . furniture around.

D I did that in my house. . . .

B I did . . . I thought it looked awful where it was, you know.

A But I . . . what annoys me is my room . . . is my room. . . . If . . . if it's in a muddle I know where everything is . . . I like my room to be in a mess.

B But you see, we . . . I keep that as a sort of main bedroom, you know . . .
(main room . . .) Yes, sometimes I don't even sleep in my room, it's so
cold. . . .

C Ooh, crumbs!

B How do you feel on this subject, Pamela?

D [with a great guffaw] Negative!

C I always know where everything is in my room even if it is untidy, but
my mother comes along and I can't find anything anywhere.

A I like it when you get to that age where your parents seem to realize that
you're . . . you're going off on your own . . . (Yes . . . You're growing
up . . .) . . . you've got your own life to lead, so you think, Right, we'll
leave all her things, she can do what she likes with them. It's her time,
she can do what she likes with her time.

B They start from a certain point, don't they?

E Well, I don't think they always do that. . . . They try to remember that
you're growing up and then they forget.

D Yes . . . they try to protect you. . . .

E They're treating you like children and telling you where to put things. . . .

C . . . going round tidying up after you.

(*Language, the Learner and the School*)

in a muddle: untidy, disorganized
Ooh, crumbs!: an exclamation

She's leaving home

Wednesday morning at five o'clock as the day begins
Silently closing her bedroom door
Leaving the note that she hoped would say more
She goes downstairs to the kitchen clutching her handkerchief.
Quietly turning the back-door key
Stepping outside she is free.

She's leaving home
We gave her most of our lives
Sacrificed most of our lives
We gave her everything money could buy
She's leaving home after living alone for so many years.

Father snores as his wife gets into her dressing-gown
Picks up the letter that's lying there
Standing alone at the top of the stairs
She breaks down and cries to her husband 'Daddy, our baby's gone!
Why should she treat us so thoughtlessly?
How could she do this to me?'

She's leaving home
We never thought of ourselves
Never a thought for ourselves
We struggled hard all our lives to get by
She's leaving home after living alone for so many years.

Friday morning at nine o'clock she is far away
Waiting to keep the appointment she made
Meeting a man from the motor-trade.

She's leaving home
What did we do that was wrong?
We didn't know it was wrong
Fun is the one thing that money can't buy
Something inside that was always denied for so many years.

John Lennon and Paul McCartney

clutching: holding tightly
to get by: to manage to live on not much money

*"Deep down she is a kind and considerate
daughter—she's gone!"*

Problem post

Dear Marje,
I'm 15 and I often see a boy on the bus when
I go home from work. I always try to sit by him
because I like him very much, but he won't have
anything to do with me. I work in a fish and
chip shop, and can never seem to get rid of the
smell. Do you think this is the trouble?

(Letter in *Woman's Mirror*)

*

I am an Indian, aged 19, and I'm in love with
a 15-year-old Eurasian schoolgirl. I fell in
love with her when she was 13, but I was

forced to 'break off' with her recently. The reasons for this are (1) She does not seem to care for me of late; (2) She has started to mix up with a set of bad girls; (3) She thinks she can boss everybody. Also I have a suspicion that she thinks I love someone else. Have I done right by breaking away from her? What shall I do?

UNCLE JOE'S REPLY: I am getting rather 'fed up' with people who keep on writing on both sides of the paper, as you have done. The next time anybody does this, I'm going to throw his letter into the waste-paper basket and say nothing.

(*Singapore Free Press*)

of late: recently

*

It's so embarrassing

I have a horrible problem, and I hope you can tell me what is wrong. You see, whenever a boy talks to me, I go scarlet, I begin to shake and sweat and my mouth goes horribly dry. It is very embarrassing and I can't speak. I am 15 and I have never been out with a boy, but I very much want to. At school, most of the boys tease me, I don't know what I'm going to do, please help me.
Mandy, Uxbridge.

You're suffering from a very, very common disease — it's called shyness! We know it won't help to cure it, but we do hope it will make you feel a little easier in your mind if we say that lots of people suffer from feeling shy and self-conscious.
Usually, people grow out of this phase but many people learn to conquer it, by forcing themselves to talk to people, to go out and meet strangers, to go to places on their own where they don't know anyone. You see, when you start growing up,

you suddenly become aware of yourself, you start taking notice of the way you look, and what other people think of you — which is good and healthy. But it often leads to those crippling feelings of self-consciousness which you will learn to come to terms with in time. Don't worry about being 'abnormal' — you aren't, you are very, very normal; lots of people you meet are shy, too, although they may not seem like it to you! Try treating boys just like other human beings, and you'll soon stop blushing and shaking every time one talks to you.

(Letter in *OK Magazine*)

scarlet: bright red
tease me: laugh at me
feeling self-conscious: feeling as if everybody is looking critically at you
phase: period in a person's development
conquer: overcome, defeat
come to terms with: understand and deal with
blushing: going red in the face

*

I am going to advise you not to pay any attention to all the different advice you are being given.

(*Woman's Weekly*)

Lover from the past

'Susan!' a man's voice said, as I was following the waiter to a table.

My heart jumped into my throat. *It can't be*, I thought. But I could never forget that voice. Whirling round, I was face-to-face with Bob Carlton.

For a frantic moment I wondered if I was about to faint. I was breathing hard, my chest rising and falling as if I'd been running up a steep hill. Bob was more handsome now than I remembered him, his shoulders broader. his features finely chiselled, the dark eyes gazing at me as if he wanted to search into my soul.

'Susan.' He repeated my name, leaving his chair and coming over to where I was standing. Ahead, the waiter glanced back, but I paid no attention. Bob and I might as well have been alone on a mountain top.

'I – I'm about to have lunch', I mumbled unsteadily, feeling the need to say something. To say *anything*.

'Then join me.'

When I nodded, he cupped one palm under my elbow, guiding me to his table. My flesh burned from his touch, despite the thickness of my coat. It had been more than two years since I'd last seen Bob and I'd assured myself a thousand times that I was 'over' him, but now I didn't know what to believe.

(From a story in *Hers*)

whirling: turning quickly
finely chiselled: smooth and straight
mumbled: said unclearly

" *You have beautiful eyes, Veronica.*"

Dating Services

(Advertisements in *Time Out*)

dating: arranging meetings, or going out regularly, with boy- or girlfriends
SAE, s.a.e.: stamped addressed envelope

"How about Thursday night, then?"

(*Daily Mirror*)

(Advertisements in *Time Out*)

dozy: sleepy
gay: (slang) homosexual
loaded: (slang) very rich

Keith Hallam

Keith Hallam is a university student of nineteen. He has shoulder-length hair, rectangular glasses and wears a black and lilac parti-coloured jacket and flared denim trousers. It is a wet Saturday night. The bright arc of light-bulbs of an amusement arcade in central London is mirrored smudgily in the wet pavement. Keith is damp and forlorn, and exudes an air of quiet despair.

I don't know why it's called gay, I think it's the most miserable thing in the world. I've known I was, ever since I was about thirteen or fourteen, but it was only when I came to London last year that I was able to express myself sexually. The trouble is that it's prevented me from doing anything else, work especially. I haven't done enough work. I've just done my exams, I expect I've failed. It's a mistake to think that being liberated means getting all the sexual experience you can. There has to be some kind of balance. If I fail, I shall have to leave university. I don't know what I'll do then. I don't know how homosexuals form relationships. I don't have any. Of all the people I've met this year, I should think only one or two have wanted to see me again, and they're always the ones I didn't particularly like. I've been into drugs, only the soft ones, but that's an isolating experience too. I don't have any friends at college, and sharing drug experiences with them isn't my idea of what a relationship should be. I know I'm quite attractive superficially; a lot of people are interested in me, but it always wears off when they find out what I'm really like.

I'm a classic case really. My mother wanted a girl. We're working-class.

I'm the apple of my mother's eye, which makes me sad. It's a kind of responsibility I can't live up to. Sometimes I stop and think that what I do is against the law, as I'm under twenty-one. I don't worry about that – I find it difficult enough to get by from day to day, without adding to my anxieties by stupid things like that. Before I came to London, I had all these fantasies about finding myself and being free to associate with whoever I chose. It's turned out to be something else. It's a kind of compulsion – the more sex you have, the more you think you need. If you ever find yourself on your own – and I do an awful lot of the time – there's only one thing to do, and that's go and look for someone to pick up. You can sleep with as many people as you like, and still be lonely as hell. Going back home on the night buses, lying awake on the edge of somebody's single bed waiting till the tubes start so you can get out, making vague promises to meet again, people you can't stand the sight of the next morning. You eat perfunctory breakfasts and say unenthusiastic hellos to other people's flatmates, a succession of faceless Adrians and Peters and Julians. It's no way to live, honestly.

(Jeremy Seabrook, *Loneliness*)

flared trousers: with the bottoms wider than the tops
arc: part of a circle
smudgily: unclearly
forlorn: lost-looking
exudes: gives out

gay: (slang) homosexual
wears off: disappears
get by: manage to live
compulsion: very powerful need
tubes: underground trains
perfunctory: hurried

St Valentine's Day

[It is an old English custom to send a message or card to the person you love on St Valentine's day (14 February). Here are some Valentine messages from *The Times*.]

SUSAN HARBERT. Thanks for: 14 good years, 5,000 breakfasts, 5 kids, and you.——Love Wally.

I CANNOT AFFORD enough space to tell you how much I love you. Will try to tell you tonight. I love you more than when you were reading the last sentence.——Love from a flower sender.

JANE, JANE, JANE, Jane, Jane, Jane, Jane, Jane, Jane, Jane, Jane, Jane, Jane, Jane, Jane.

MARY MY DARLING. I love you madly. I am so happy to have you as my valentine——Michael.

TO KATIE CAT. Hoping this will make you purr with pleasure.——Lauremok.

SUKI. I'm a fool to fall for you, but here in the morning light, tell me how can love be wrong and feel so right ? ————Malc.

WENDY——Thank you for your patience, love and support during the last few months. With all my love Barrie.

CHARLES SIDNEY HUNT——May you have that which you deserve—— ME ! !

FLIP.——Happy birthday. Hope you didn't buy this left-wing rubbish.

TO BIG FEET from Baby Blue Eyes ——especially today.

ROSES ARE RED, violets are blue, sugar is sweet, and I love Prue.

(*The Times*)

113

Margo and the spring

Margo was always badly affected by the spring. Her personal appearance, always of absorbing interest to her, now became almost an obsession. Piles of freshly laundered clothes filled her bedroom, while the washing-line sagged under the weight of clothes newly washed. Singing shrilly and untunefully she would drift about the villa, carrying piles of flimsy underwear or bottles of scent. She would seize every opportunity to dive into the bathroom, in a swirl of white towels, and once in there she was as hard to dislodge as a limpet from a rock. The family in turn would bellow and batter on the door, getting no more satisfaction than an assurance that she was nearly finished, an assurance which we had learnt by bitter experience not to have any faith in. Eventually she would emerge, glowing and immaculate, and drift from the house, humming, to sun-bathe in the olive-groves or go down to the sea and swim.

(Gerald Durrell, *My Family and Other Animals*)

absorbing: fascinating
sagged: hung down
shrilly: in a high, rather hard voice
drift: move dreamily
villa: country house
flimsy: delicate
swirl: quick circular movement
dislodge: remove
limpet: kind of shellfish that sticks very tightly to a rock
bellow: shout
batter: bang
emerge: come out
immaculate: perfectly clean
humming: 'singing' without opening the mouth
olive-groves: groups of olive trees

'I have found that if you don't lock the bathroom some people are taking baths every day.'
– Mr J. Glenton, member of Morecambe Hotels and Caterers Association, during a discussion on bathing habits of holiday visitors.

(*Morecambe Guardian*)

To get married you have to shave you're legs. I think

Alice aged 5

115

How much do we touch each other?

[In 1966, psychologists carried out a survey to find out how much British people touch each other. The diagrams below illustrate the results, showing how much people are touched (and where) by their parents and friends.]

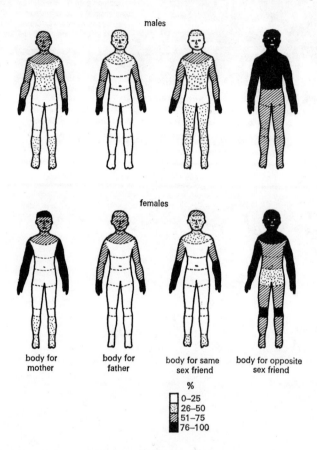

males

females

| body for mother | body for father | body for same sex friend | body for opposite sex friend |

%
□ 0–25
▨ 26–50
▧ 51–75
■ 76–100

(Michael Argyle, *The Psychology of Interpersonal Behaviour*)

Head and face massage

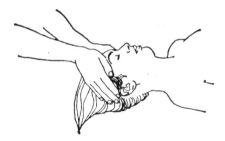

1 ★ Before anything else I like to hold my
palms lightly against my friend's forehead for a few moments. Cover the forehead
with the heels of your hands, letting the
fingers extend down the temples. Apply no
pressure. Pause as long as seems right and
comfortable to you: a few seconds, half a
minute, whatever. Centre yourself. Let your
friend grow accustomed to your touch.

2 ★ Now begin massaging you friend's forehead with
the balls of your thumbs. First mentally divide the
forehead into horizontal strips about a half an inch wide.
Then, starting with your thumbs at the centre of the forehead
just below the hairline, glide both thumbs at once in either

direction outwards along the topmost strip. Press moderately: use about the pressure it takes to stick a stamp on an envelope. Continue all the way to the temples, a surprisingly sensitive place, and end there by moving your thumbs in a single circle about

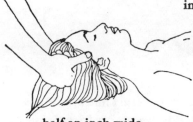

half an inch wide.

Immediately pick up your thumbs, return them to the centre of the forehead, and begin the next strip down, again moving your thumbs from the centre outwards.

Then, working progressively downwards, do each of the others in turn, ending with a strip running just above your friend's eyebrows. Remember to conclude each strip with another small circle on the temples – a flourish not strictly necessary, but your friend will feel it's very 'right'.

(George Downing, *The Massage Book*)

glide: move smoothly
temples: the places at the side of the head (above and behind the eyes) where the bone is thin

"I can't remember it's name, but it leaves mature skin supple and fresh again, is as light as a Snowflake, rich with vitamins and moisturisers, items from a base of precious natural essences, contains exclusive bio-natural extracts, is a self-pampering treatment for tired and ageing skin, and is recommended for women whose quest for beauty knows no bounds."

(*Punch*)

mature: completely adult
supple: not hard or stiff
pampering: treating very kindly

quest: search
bounds: limits

JŌVAN
musk oil
aftershave / cologne
FOR MEN.

Musk oil for men.
The provocative scent
that instinctively calms
and yet arouses your basic
animal desires.
And hers.
In an aftershave / cologne.
To take you a long way to
where it's at. To the most
pleasurable of conclusions.
Because it is powerful.
Stimulating. Unbelievable.
And yet, legal.

4 FL.OZ. 118 CC. ml

Just splash this
natural lotion on your
face, neck, chest.
After shaving.
Before anything else.
It's unmistakably male.
A no nonsense scent all
your own. With lingering
powers that will last
as long as you do.
And then some.
It may not put more
women into your life.
But it will probably put
more life into your women.
Because it's
the message lotion.
Get it on!

JŌVAN
musk oil
aftershave / cologne
FOR MEN.

CONTAINS:
SD ALCOHOL 39-C,
DEIONIZED WATER,
MEN'S MUSK OIL
FRAGRANCE, D & C
BROWN #1 REPL.,
D & C GREEN #5

REORDER JF-901
JOVAN, INC.
CHICAGO, IL. 60611
MADE IN U.S.A.
© 1973 BY JOVAN, INC.

musk: animal extract used as a base for perfumes
where it's at: where exciting things are happening
lingering: long-lasting

may i feel said he
(i'll squeal said she
just once said he)
it's fun said she

(may i touch said he
how much said she
a lot said he)
why not said she

(let's go said he
not too far said she
what's too far said he
where you are said she)

may i stay said he
(which way said she
like this said he
if you kiss said she

may i move said he
is it love said she)
if you're willing said he
(but you're killing said she

but it's life said he
but your wife said she
now said he)
ow said she

(tiptop said he
don't stop said she
oh no said he)
go slow said she

(cccome? said he
ummm said she)
you're divine! said he
(you are Mine said she)

e. e. cummings

squeal: give a small scream
ow: exclamation of pain
tiptop: wonderful
come: (here) reach a sexual climax, have an orgasm

"*No. I'm not in the mood any more . . .*"

(*Punch*)

I've been going steady with my boyfriend for two years and we both intend getting engaged – we're both 19. He says he'll never marry a girl who's not a virgin and so to be sure that I am one he wants to have intercourse with me before we become engaged.

(Letter in *Woman's Own*)

going steady: going out regularly
have intercourse: make love, have sex

Dear Marje,
If a girl has intercourse and then has nothing more to do with boys for a year, can she become a virgin again?
(*July 3*)

(Letter signed 'Hopeful' in *Woman's Mirror*)

One young man's attitude to sex

I mean, you lead your own life from the age of about sixteen, or you should
do. Anybody else who tries to rule your life at sixteen: well, you can't do it.
I mean, you learn off your mistakes, because if you do what everybody else
tells you, you never know if you're going to do it right. Not just sex, but life
altogether. But sex comes into everybody's life by the time you're about
sixteen. I mean, they're maturing more. . . . I mean, you see women going
round, about fourteen, and, I mean, well they're mature. Well, they weren't
like that before. And the older people think it's wrong. But it's . . .
everything is changing. Like I say, life's changing. They can't understand.
It's changing a lot faster. Since the war it's changed that fast, they haven't
been able to keep up with it. We're going into it, and we've got to accept it
straightway, from the very start. And you work your way into it, you play
around, and then you find your way into it. It's bloody normal. We're not
sex maniacs. . . . You go out for a drink, and you expect to finish up with a
tart, you know. Not just for sex, just to finish the night off. Make it a good
night. It's only bloody normal. I mean, now, nineteen, twenty, twenty-one,
that's the sort of ages we are now. Well, I think we know enough about
bloody sex to keep us going. I mean, we're not ignorant on the subject, and
we're not too far-fetched on it. You know, we don't get right excited every
time we see a bloody woman walking down the street, but if you get a
girl . . . it's just like they say. It takes bloody two of 'em. And a girl goes on
it more than a lad does, she'll make it more obvious to the lad, because
they're weakest, they can't hide what they're feeling. They're weaker when
it comes to sex. Women can't live without sex. They can't pretend to.
I mean, it's more emotional to them. You know, it's more within them.
I mean, a bloke, they can do it like that, and they don't think any more of it,
but a girl has to. With a lad, he hasn't got to go through what she has, when
it's finished, it's finished for him more or less. But for a girl it carries on for
another bloody nine months. But with a lad (*he snaps his fingers*), he can't
help it. It's just life.

(Jeremy Seabrook, *City Close-Up*)

maturing: becoming adult
that fast: so fast
tart: (slang) girl
far-fetched: (here) obsessed, abnormal
lad: boy
bloke: (slang) man

Two girls talking about love and sex

JANICE: Love? Well, I don't know what the word means. To me, I'm not sure that it really means anything. Well, it hasn't so far in my life. Not love for a person of my age or a similar age. Love for my parents, yes, but. . . .

TINA: What about that boy you were going out with? You said you were in love with him.

JANICE: Oh yes, that was because he'd brainwashed me into thinking I was in love with him. Whereas all the time I wasn't. But now I've got everything straight about that. I know that kind of thing won't ever happen again. But when love does come along, I shall know.

TINA: Yes, it's usually if the boy keeps saying he loves you, you tend to say it back sometimes, but you don't mean it. And then you get to a pitch where you daren't not say it, but all the time you don't mean it. . . . And when they realize, they can't understand. 'You said you loved me.' But you daren't say you didn't, because that just proves you're a liar.

JANICE: I'd never say that now. Really, you know, it's taught me an awful lot. I feel that going out with that boy for so long has made me very mature in my ideas about love now, and relationships. I learnt a lot from the experience. . . . What I really learnt was that the word 'love' is used too loosely. I learnt what to expect from a relationship, and now I'm using what I've learnt with the boy I'm going out with now.

TINA: As soon as the word 'love' comes into a relationship, everything starts going haywire.

JANICE: People don't realize that you could just go out with somebody, to go out with them, to enjoy their company. But it's never like that. It's always something more complicated. People make things more complicated than what they are. They enjoy doing it.

TINA: They try to define relationships when there's no need to.

Is sex before marriage wrong?

JANICE: I don't think sex before marriage is wrong. Anybody who has had sex before marriage, I wouldn't say anything against them. It's just their personal belief. I don't think I'd have sex before marriage unless I loved the person.

TINA: Yes, but how can you tell whether they love you or not? You get a lot of these boys who say they love a girl just to get into bed with her, and when she says yes they go running to the hair shops or chemist's, or wherever it is, to get the contraceptives, and then, two weeks after, they don't want to know the girl. I think this is a sign of immaturity.

JANICE: Why? Why is it any different whether you do it before you're married or not? It's the same act whether you're married or not. The only reason I wouldn't have sex before marriage is because I don't want to have a kid. If you don't believe in God, are you married when you sign a piece of paper, or are you married when you know your husband?

(Jeremy Seabrook, *City Close-Up*)

brainwashed: persuaded, convinced
a pitch: a point
haywire: crazy
contraceptives: things used to prevent pregnancy

Can you hear me, Mother?

BRRR . . BRRR . . BRRR . . BRRR . . CLICK!

  'Hello, Mum? It's me.'

  '*Me!* Mike.'

  '*Mike!* M . . I . . K . . Your son! Yes, that's right. That's Mike.'

  'No, I'm fine, nothing's wrong.'

  'Look, why shouldn't I ring you up? I know it's six months since you last heard from me, but. . . .'

  'Yes, I suppose you did think I was dead. I'm sorry.'

  'Look, if you just go on and on like this, I'll put the phone down, and then you won't hear my news.'

  'No, I'm not married.'

  'No, I'm not in trouble. Why does it always have to be one or the other?'

  'Well, I don't take after my Father in every way, you know. How is Dad, by the way?'

  'Well, you should visit him more often, you know. He's due out in a few months' time, isn't he?'

  'Well, just tell the blasted lodger he'll have to go. Look, I don't want to know about all that, I've got something important to tell you. Look, I've met this girl. . . .'

  'I don't know. . . .'

  'I don't know because I haven't asked her.'

  'All right. All right, next time I see her, I'll just walk right up to her, and say 'Hello, darling, is your Father rich?' Will that satisfy you?'

  'Look, I was just joking Mother, I'm going to do nothing of the kind. Actually, I don't care how much money she's got. I love her.'

  'I said I love her.'

  'No, I have not been drinking. . . .'

  'No, she's not up the spout, as you so delicately put it Mother. For heaven's sake. . . .'

  'Yes, Mum, of course you are going to meet her. Actually she's dying to meet you, too. I've told her all about you.'

'No, of course I didn't tell her all about you and the vicar. . . .'

'Because I never tell anyone about you and the vicar. . . .'

'Because I am ashamed of you and the vicar, that's why! I've told you before, it doesn't make it any better, him being a vicar. If anything, it makes it worse. Listen, I told her the good bits about you. That didn't take long, either. Ha ha ha.'

'Oh don't start crying, for heaven's sake, Mum. It was just a joke.'

'All right, I'm sorry.'

'Yes, very, very, very, very sorry. All right? Listen, don't you want to meet her?'

'Right. Splendid. Shall I bring her to tea?'

'Yes, I know you don't have tea at home. But couldn't you just for once pretend to have tea?'

'Oh, all right then, I'll bring her to gin as usual. But could you try at least to create a good impression?'

'You know exactly what I mean. Put the empties somewhere else, for a start. And the coal.'

'Yes, and the lodger, too.'

'Listen Mum. Please, please, whatever else you do, please don't do your trick. It's cruel to the goldfish.'

'OK, Mum, thank you, that's very nice of you. Mum, just one more thing. Will Aunt Alice be there?'

'Oh dear, will she? Well, let me put it like this, Mum – has the treatment worked?'

'Mum, my girl will *not* understand. People do not understand that some people think they are Marie-Antoinette and go around throwing cake at other people.'

'Oh, it's Boadicea, is it? That's an improvement, I must say. What does she throw?'

'Spears? Look Mum, I don't think I'll bother to bring her home to meet you after all. I'll just tell her what I tell everyone else.'

'That I'm an orphan, of course.'

(Mike Russell, *OK Magazine*)

take after: resemble
he's due out: he's going to be let out of prison
blasted: a swearword (not very strong)
lodger: person who rents a room
up the spout: (slang) pregnant
empties: empty bottles

The world's most complex machine

What is the biggest and most complex machine in the world today ? The question was posed recently by Professor Colin Cherry of Imperial College, London.

He went on to argue that the answer was not a computer, not Concorde, not a North Sea oil platform—it was the global telephone network. Large continental networks, linked together by submarine cables and satellite connexions, together form a working machine of unimaginable size and complexity, Professor Cherry said.

This week James Merriman, Post Office board member for technology, gave scale to this concept: the global telecommunications system embraced 350 million telephones in more than 50 countries, representing an investment of about £50,000m.

"Some 200 million of these telephones", Mr Merriman added, "can already intercommunicate directly and automatically without human intervention."

A big machine, indeed, and one whose development was begun 100 years ago this week by Alexander Graham Bell. "Mr Watson, come here ; I want to see you" was the first intelligible sentence conveyed by a telephone, from Bell to his assistant, on March 10, 1876.

(Kenneth Owen, *The Times*)

global: world-wide
network: connected system
linked: connected
gave scale to this concept: showed how large it was

"I repeat, this is the early
morning call you requested."

Crossed lines

[Letters to the editor of *The Times*.]

(*July 3*)

Sir, A year or two ago you published a letter
from me, in which I claimed -- and, I think,
established – a record; I had got a crossed line
on which I heard a man getting a wrong number.

I think I now have another record to
announce: I have just got, while ringing *The
Times*, simultaneous reception of the ringing
tone, the engaged tone and someone else's
conversation.

Yours truly,
BERNARD LEVIN

(*July 4*)

Sir, Loath as I am to break any record set up
by Mr Bernard Levin, I think I can beat him
in the field of telephone athletics.

The other day, while attempting to telephone the Savoy hotel, I encountered two crossed lines: a gentleman trying to place a bet with his bookmaker suddenly found himself talking to a ladies' hairdresser in Fulham. The three of us, however, held a genial conversation on the decline of public amenities.

This was projected against a background of an engaged signal, a dialling tone, indiscriminate 'pips', as well as what sounded suspiciously like heavy breathing.

Yours faithfully,
PAUL CALLAN

(*July 13*)
Sir, With reference to the letters of Mr Bernard Levin and Mr Paul Callan regarding crossed lines, may I tell you that a short while ago I also had a crossed line, and, as Mr Callan found, the other man was making a bet with his bookmaker – in actual fact £7 to win on As Friendly.

I told various friends of this and we immediately placed similar bets on this horse, which came in first at 3 to 1 in the 4.15 at Epsom.

May I, therefore, thank the Post Office telecommunications department for their excellent service.

Yours faithfully,
EDGAR MEHL

crossed line: fault on a telephone line which enables you to hear other people's conversation
simultaneous: at the same time
loath: unwilling
bookmaker: man who accepts bets on race-horses, etc.
genial: friendly
decline: falling standards
dialling tone: the noise a telephone makes to tell you that you can dial a number
the 4.15: the race at 4.15 p.m.

'Well, if I Called the Wrong Number, Why Did You Answer the Phone?'

Nervous disorders of telephones

A subscriber on a New Forest exchange complained that his phone rang every time the lavatory chain was pulled. The complaint proved true, reports the GPO magazine, and the chain reaction has now been put right.

(*Daily Express*)

subscriber: telephone user
exchange: (area served by) telephone exchange
GPO: General Post Office

My morbid interest in the Philosophy and Technology of the Telephone continues. Did you see not long back that there is a man in the New Forest whose telephone rings every time he flushes the lavatory? I have the cutting filed somewhere under 'Telephones, Nervous Disorders of'. Though if it turns out to be also the case that the lavatory flushes every time the telephone rings, I may have to change the diagnosis. Flushing whenever the phone rings – I guess that's just love.

Anyway, no amateur of the telephone has time to be bored. The other day a team of cerebral looking men came down our road and made fine expert adjustments to the telephone cable, as a result of which the wire was disconnected from my telephone and connected to the telephone of an entirely different subscriber. Fastidious as ever, I complained about this, and the engineers reconnected me – adding, without extra charge, the wire formerly leading to the other subscriber's phone, so that I got all the calls for both of us.

I felt horribly mean when I complained about this generous arrangement. But the Post Office were most polite and helpful, and sent round another team of men who radically readjusted the whole system once again – so that I got all this other man's calls and he got all mine. It went on like this for three days. Oh, we all enjoyed it, really – though I have to be careful about my blood-pressure now.

Michael Frayn

morbid: unhealthy, sick
flush: (1) pull the chain to let the water wash out a lavatory pan, (2) go red in the face
amateur: person interested in
cerebral: very intelligent
fastidious: fussy about small details

> The automatic flushing system of a 'gents' at Totnes (Devon) Guildhall will be stopped when the Queen visits the town on 27 July – so that the noise does not disturb the Royal party. It has also been suggested that guests should stand in a semi-circle – to hide the entrance.
>
> (*Sunday Pictorial*)

'gents': men's lavatory

New loo is only flush in the pan

Railwaymen, like so many of us, have to pay a call from time to time, and this is equally true if you are locked up in a little box all day, looking after the level crossing.

That is what Mr Clarence Page does. He looks after the West River Crossing, a couple of miles south of Ely, in Cambridgeshire. He has to pay a call from time to time.

In the past, the toilets in the box have been rather primitive, necessitating regular trips into the fields for emptying. The box at West River Crossing used to be a signal box, and is well equipped with heating, running water and even a cooker. But the sanitary facilities were below standard.

Mr Page, who is on the Local Departmental Committee of his union, contacted British Rail area headquarters in Norwich and asked them if they would consider fitting an up-to-the-minute twentieth-century flush toilet

They said no, but they would put in a new chemical toilet. Mr Page pointed out that there had been three of those in his box over the past six years – he has worked in it for ten years and been on the railways 47 years – and it seemed to him an unnecessary expense when a flush toilet would last for generations.

Anyway, he had this friend, Mr

Ron Angel, who was a local builder – built Mr and Mrs Page's bungalow in Littleport, in fact – who would do the complete job, pan, plumbing, tank, cistern and all the other accoutrements of modern sanitation, for a mere £25. Clarence and Ron were friends.

But Norwich had said no, so Mr Page left it a while and then had a word with the new local manager. How about a cheap flush toilet, he asked? This manager went away for a think and then came back and said fine.

Mr Ron Angel got to work, at the original price, did a beautiful job, and Mr Page and his colleagues at West River Crossing were happy with their convenient new convenience.

Word got back to Norwich. They were not pleased. They got on to the local office and arranged for a team of British Rail men to go along to the West River Crossing box and remove Ron Angel's flush toilet.

It happened on a Monday morning, on Mr Page's rest day. They took the flush apart and fitted a chemical toilet.

'I really couldn't tell you what Clarence said when he found out', said Mrs Beryl Page, his wife, who has herself been on the railways 25 years, and also runs a level crossing, a different one, with a box with a flush toilet in it.

'It seemed a shame, and a waste of money. I'm not sure what the chemical ones cost, but they say it's as much as £200.'

(Peter Cole, *The Guardian*)

loo: (slang) lavatory
flush in the pan: a play on words, typical of this newspaper (flushing is pulling the chain ✷ or pressing the handle to wash out a lavatory pan; a flash in the pan is something that lasts for a very short time)
pay a call: go to the lavatory
level crossing: place where a road and railway line cross (usually protected by gates)
sanitary facilities: lavatory   *accoutrements:* special equipment
plumbing: water pipes   *convenience:* lavatory

Theft of railway station alleged

A man was accused yesterday of stealing a town's railway station. Mr Michael Meredith, prosecuting at Wakefield (Yorkshire) Crown Court, said that Mr Reginald S——— (33), demolished the buildings, took up track, and sold the materials.

Mr S———, demolition contractor of Dewsbury, pleaded not guilty to stealing nearly 24 tons of metal including railway lines, stone and timber belonging to British Railways.

Mr Meredith said that Cleckheaton Station had been closed for some time and British Railways accepted the tender of a Leeds firm to clear the site.

The firm was to get £2,382 and the proceeds from the sale of materials, expected to be about £600. But before the firm could start work it was discovered the station had to a large extent already been demolished.

Mr S——— admitted he was responsible but claimed he had been hired to do the job by a Mr. W——— of Northern Sites Development in Leeds.

'The prosecution say neither exist and that S———'s story is a lie', Mr Meredith said.

(Newspaper report)

demolished: knocked down
track: railway lines
timber: wood used in building

tender: offer to do a job for a certain price
site: land which has been, or will be, built on

Men had to buy tickets to chase a mugger

Three men chased a "mugger" into East Putney station, London, after he punched and kicked an elderly woman, but were turned back at the barrier because they had no tickets, it was stated at the Central Criminal Court yesterday.

They were refused use of a telephone to call the police, so they bought platform tickets, went into the station and caught the attacker, a youth of 17. One of the pursuers had to go outside to make a 999 call.

Mr Justice Melford Stevenson said the incident deserved to be brought to the attention of the railway authorities. He sent the mugger to jail for five years.

Terry Taylor, of Pendle Road, Furzedown, London, earlier had admitted assaulting Mrs Margaret Percy, aged 67, with intent to rob her.

Mr Robin Wilde, for the prosecution, said that when Mrs Percy screamed, Taylor put his hand to her mouth, knocking her teeth out.

(*The Times*)

mugger: person who robs people in the street, using violence
999 call: emergency telephone call to the police
assaulting: attacking

A mugger's point of view

[From an interview with a mugger.]

No, I don't look on it as immoral. They go home to their nice little house, don't they, after I've taken their wallet off them? They sit in front of their television all comfy on their sofa.

Where's *my* television set, I ask you? where's *my* three-piece suite, no matter how many cheap little wallets I might ever happen to nick? . . .

But I never hurt anyone. Never. Not if I can help it. If I do lay one on a cat because he tries to have a go at me, I'm really gentle. I smack him about a bit. I try to get him on the ground, and then I kick him a little bit just to keep him laying there while I get away. . . .

They deserve it, anyway – everything they get and more. They think they're so high and mighty when you first come up to them.

(*Daily Mail*)

comfy: (slang) comfortable
three-piece suite: sofa and two armchairs in the same style
nick: (slang) steal
lay one on a cat: (slang) hit a person
high and mighty: superior

If your Colour TV 📺 goes up in smoke or robbers roll out your much-prized 🧿➡ Persian carpet, you'll feel a lot happier with **replacement as new.** If your roof 🏠 is raised in a Force 8 gale, your carelessness causes a 🏍 nasty spill or you fracture a fibula while 🔧 decorating, you'll feel a lot happier 🐦 with really effective protection. You can get it all in one complete insurance policy

MasterCover

Just send us the coupon today. Or talk to your broker.

fracture: break
fibula: a bone in the leg
broker: a 'go-between' who puts customers in touch with insurance companies

135

If you have your car stolen, you could be unlucky enough to get it back.

Most car thefts are the work of amateurs. People looking for kicks, not for profit.

They'll steal your car and take it for a joy-ride, to the coast, a pop concert, to or from a party.

Then they'll leave it. Not as they found it, but modified. The bodywork crumpled or, even worse, a complete write-off.

Getting it back is sometimes a bigger shock than having it stolen.

Over a quarter of a million cars were stolen last year – that's one every two minutes. Most of them taken by amateurs. Most of them because they were not secured properly.

It's the popular family car they're after. Usually five years old or more - one that won't get noticed in a crowd.

The most likely places are quiet residential streets, outside your own home. The most likely times are after 6 pm on Fridays and Saturdays.

So don't say it can't happen to you.

It can.

And if it does, you're in for some shocks.

If you make a claim on your insurance, you'll most likely lose your no-claims bonus. And the way car prices are today, you may find yourself a lot worse off all round.

So cut down the chances of your car being stolen. Always check that all doors are locked and all windows fastened. Don't leave valuables in your car. If you have to - lock them away in the boot. Fit an anti-theft device, and use it. And never leave your keys in the ignition, even if you're just popping in for a paper.

Remember, it only takes a minute to steal your car, and less than a minute to secure it.

Lock it or lose it.

Lock all doors, secure all windows, lock all valuables away in the boot.

Issued by H.M. Government

---

amateurs: not professionals
for kicks: for fun
a complete write-off: too badly damaged to repair
secured: locked up
you're in for some shocks: you're going to have some shocks
no-claims bonus: reduction of, for example, 60 per cent in the cost of insurance for a person who has not claimed money from the insurance company for an accident
worse off: poorer

modified: changed
crumpled: damaged

IT WILL REASSURE YOU WHEN YOU NEED IT.

IT WILL HELP RESTORE YOUR CONFIDENCE SHOULD IT EVER DESERT YOU.

IT WILL SOOTHE AND SOLACE YOU AFTER A HECTIC DAY.

IT WILL INSULATE YOU FROM THE NOISE AND CHAOS OF THE OUTSIDE WORLD.

IT WILL REBUILD YOUR MORALE; YOUR AMBITIONS.

BUT MOST OF ALL, IT WILL REMIND YOU THAT YOUR LIFE HAS NOT BEEN TOTALLY WITHOUT SUCCESS.

[Newspaper advertisement for Jaguar cars]

soothe and solace: relax and comfort
hectic: fast and busy

Why do the British drive on the left?

The heart is (or, to be exact, appears to be) on the left side of the body. In the more primitive forms of warfare some type of shield is therefore used to protect the left side, leaving the offensive weapon to be held in the right hand. The normal offensive weapon was the sword, worn in a scabbard or sheath. If the sword was to be wielded in the right hand, the scabbard would have to be worn on the left side. With a scabbard worn on the left, it became physically impossible to mount a horse on the off side unless intending to face the tail – which was not the normal practice. But if you mount on the near side, you will want to have your horse on the left of the road, so that you are clear of the traffic while mounting. It therefore becomes natural and proper to keep to the left, the contrary practice (as adopted in some backward countries) being totally opposed to all the deepest historical instincts. Free of arbitrary traffic rules the normal human being swings to the left.

(C. Northcote Parkinson, *Parkinson's Law*)

warfare: war
the off side: the right side
arbitrary: decided for no good reason

> Ghana is to change over to driving on the right. The change will be made gradually.
>
> (Ghana paper)

> Sir, – Traffic over the Channel bridge from England to France should proceed on the right, so as to prepare the drivers for the conditions they will meet when they arrive in France. Conversely, traffic from France to England should proceed on the left.
> Yours truly,
> DEREK E. COX
>
> (*The Times*)

" Bump the green one, Perkins."

Woman, 86, hurt in collision

Two killed on fogbound motorways

Daily Mail, Tuesday, January 4, 1977

Ian, five, falls from car as it speeds along the fast lane

PC races to snatch boy from motorway death

Three die on M6

Boy, eight, victim of road crash

Ice, fog hamper drivers

Car demolished cottage door

Motor cyclist dies in multiple crash

collision: crash
fogbound: covered in fog
M6: a motorway
hamper: make things difficult for
demolished: knocked down

Epidemic on wheels

Deaths and injuries from motor-vehicle accidents are reaching epidemic proportions in developing countries around the world, according to the World Health Organization. Traffic accidents in the young nations of Africa amount to a 'social scourge', and all too often the victims are young, educated Africans whose increased earning power has enabled them to buy a motorcycle or an automobile. Statistics from three Latin-American countries, Chile, Costa Rica and Venezuela, reveal that, as in the US, traffic accidents have become the leading cause of death among young adults.

About 250,000 people throughout the world are killed in traffic accidents each year, and more than seven million are injured. Although the US has the highest number of people killed in traffic accidents of any country (about 50,000 per year), it has one of the lowest rates of fatalities per motor vehicle or passenger mile. For example, in the US there are six fatalities per 100 million passenger miles, whereas in Kenya and Uganda there are from 55 to 65 fatalities per 100 million passenger miles. In India the fatality rate per motor vehicle is 10 to 15 times higher than it is in the US. In all countries the death rate from traffic accidents is higher for males than it is for females.

The majority of developing countries have a higher incidence of traffic accidents involving pedestrians than of accidents involving motor vehicles alone. Among the causes, the WHO reports, are poor roads, pedestrian ignorance of road signs, lack of instruction in the use of roads and heavy pedestrian and bicycle traffic on the roads.

To combat the growing epidemic of traffic accidents, the WHO has undertaken a worldwide epidemiological study of road traffic accidents and is encouraging the development of preventive programmes. 'If traffic accidents are tackled by methods similar to those used against the great killing diseases', the organization states, 'the present epidemic of road deaths could be made to disappear just as plague and smallpox have now been eliminated almost everywhere in the world.'

(*Scientific American*)

epidemic: very widespread illness, disease
scourge: something that causes suffering
fatalities: deaths
plague, smallpox: two serious infectious diseases

Road accidents

Number of deaths, by type of road user: Great Britain

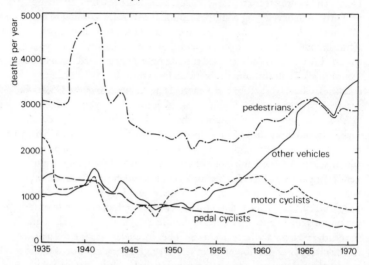

Deaths among the four main classes of road users are shown here, and the figures include all deaths except for persons who die more than one month after the accident, in which case they are included in the figures for injured, not for killed.

Motor cyclists include riders of mopeds and scooters and their passengers, and the category of 'other vehicles' includes drivers and passengers of cars and goods vehicles.

The striking feature of the series is that, in spite of the enormous increase in the number of vehicles on the roads, the total number of deaths is roughly the same as for 1935. In 1935 it was motor cyclists and pedestrians who bore the brunt, now it is car drivers (and their passengers) as well as pedestrians. The carnage among pedestrians that accompanied the blackout during the war is shown graphically.

The other change since 1935 is that although road *deaths* have not increased materially, the number *injured* has done so. A quarter of a million were injured each year during the 1930s; now the figure is 350,000.

The number of people killed on the roads since the turn of the century has now reached 335,000, an immense figure although modest compared to the two million lives claimed by the automobile in the United States, a total five times greater than the number of Americans killed in battle in all the wars since the beginning of this century.

The Department of the Environment, using a new basis for calculating the total cost to the community from road accidents, arrived at a figure for 1969 of £320 millions.

Although the total number of road deaths is rising slowly, this must be seen against the growth of motor traffic. The number of casualties per million vehicle-miles travelled (2·90 in 1969) has been falling steadily since the 1950s.

Source:
Annual Abstract of Statistics

(Alan F. Sillitoe, *Britain in Figures*)

moped: motorized bicycle
scooter: kind of small motor-cycle
bore the brunt: suffered most
carnage: large-scale killing
blackout: during the war, people were not allowed to show lights at night
casualties: people injured or killed

A car chase

Slush was coming up on to the windscreen and the wipers knocked it away. We made a straight run through Steglitz and Sdende because I wanted to know if they'd now make any attempt to close right up and ram. They didn't. They just wanted to know where I was going. I'd have to think of somewhere. Their sidelamps were steady in the mirror, a pair of pale fireflies floating along the perspective of the streets. We crossed the Attila-strasse and I made a dive into Ring-strasse going south-east, then braked to bring them right behind me and make them slow. As soon as they had I whipped through the gears and increased the gap to half a block before swinging sharp left into the Mariendorfdamm and heading north-east towards the Tempelhof. Then a series of dives through back-streets that got them going in earnest. The speeds were high now and I had the advantage because I could go where I liked, whereas they had to think out my moves before I made them, and couldn't, because I didn't know them myself until the last second.

They lost me once and came up broadside-on by luck at the north end of a block, and once they hit something in a slide and the sound echoed between the walls of the narrow street. They were getting worried, certain now that I must be heading for a destination that had to be kept secret.

The mount of the Kreuzberg was ahead of us and I swerved right by Flughafen station and then back-tracked because we were getting too close to the Hotel Prinz Johan and I wanted them to keep thinking I was going somewhere else, somewhere important, before I made an all-out effort to lose them and leave them guessing.

Their lights were close behind me at the Alt-Tempelhof and Tempelhof-damm crossing and then I saw them flick out. There was no tyre-squeal because of the slush; there were only a few long seconds of comparative silence before the sound of the crash filled the buildings like an explosion. I was placed in a slow drift for a right-angle when I heard it, and brought the nose round full-lock with the kerb for a cush. The impetus of the DKW had sent it back across the street in a ricochet and I saw it hit a parked Opel broadside-on in a smother of slush and debris. Then it took fire.

(Adam Hall, *The Quiller Memorandum*)

slush: melting snow
ram: hit my car with theirs
whipped through the gears: changed gear very quickly
in earnest: seriously
broadside-on: sliding sideways
swerved: suddenly changed direction
all-out: trying as hard as possible
flick out: go out suddenly
tyre-squeal: screaming noise from the tyres

drift: sideways slide
full-lock: with the steering-wheel turned as far as possible
with the kerb for a cush: with the side of the pavement to stop me
impetus: force of movement
DKW: a German make of car
ricochet: bounce
debris: broken bits

"I've got a three-litre Rover at the moment about a mile outside Salford."

(Punch)

Ambition

I got pocketed behind 7X-3824;
He was making 65, but I can do a little more.
I crowded him on the curves, but I couldn't get past,
And on the straightaways there was always some truck coming fast.
Then we got to the top of a mile-long incline
And I edged her out to the left, a little over the white line,
And ahead was a long grade with construction at the bottom,
And I said to the wife, 'Now by golly I got'm!'
I bet I did 85 going down the long grade,
And I braked her down hard in front of the barricade,
And I swung in ahead of him and landed fine
Behind 9W-7679.

Morris Bishop

pocketed: trapped
7X-3824: a car's registration number
65: 65 miles an hour
crowded: got very close to
incline: slope
her: the car
grade: slope
construction: road works
by golly I got'm: by God, I've got him

A rise of 14 per cent in deaths and serious injuries on Devon and Cornwall roads was blamed by police chiefs on the slow reactions of elderly pedestrians.

(*Plymouth Sunday Independent*)

'I want to do a ton' says speeding driver of 96

A motorist of 96 was fined £7 yesterday for speeding – his first offence in 70 years motoring.

His licence was endorsed but he was not ordered to take a driving test and his age was not mentioned in court.

Mr D———, a widower, was caught by a radar trap doing 41 m.p.h. in a 30 m.p.h. area, while travelling near his home in Folkestone, last November.

He refused to give his age to police when stopped, but later wrote a letter to a newspaper, complaining about the radar trap. He said he was 96, and hoped to 'do a ton' around Brand's Hatch, on his 100th birthday.

Mr D———, a retired docks executive, did not appear in court yesterday. He admitted the offence by letter.

After the case the chairman of the magistrates, Commander Richard Bristow, said: 'I do not wish to comment on whether or not I knew of the defendant's advanced years. No evidence was given about his age and we did not feel compelled to inquire about it.'

Police Constable William Holton, one of the men operating the radar trap, said afterwards: 'He certainly didn't look anywhere near 96. I thought he was in his middle sixties.'

Mr D——— said: 'Oh, I'm 96 all right, but I'm in good shape. I'd have been a bit upset if they'd disqualified me, but I've no doubt that I could pass any test they might have asked me to take.

'I first drove in 1902 – a motorbike. More than 70 years of trouble-free motoring is not a bad record and I've got no reason to stop thinking that I'm one of the safest drivers on the road.

'Mind you, I'm still a bit annoyed about being caught. On that particular stretch of road, 30 m.p.h. is absurd.

'I take regular medical check-ups and my heart and lungs are first-class. I do need glasses and my hearing could be better, but I've always been fit to drive.'

(*Daily Mail*)

to do a ton: (slang) to drive at 100 m.p.h.
his licence was endorsed: a record of his offence was written in his driving licence
Brand's Hatch: a race-track

METROPOLITAN POLICE

405 7921 4

Section 80-Road Traffic Regulation Act 1967
Notice of opportunity to pay fixed penalty

Motor Vehicle
Registration mark   PART 1

| X | G | O | 8 | 2 | 6 | G |

was seen in

QUEENSWAY   W2

from   to/at

| 1 | 2 | 3 | 0 | | 1 | 2 | 3 | 5 |

on the   day of

| 3 | O | | J | U | L | | 1 | 9 | 7 | 7 |

in circumstances giving me reasonable cause to

believe that the offence described at | 0 | 6 |

in PART 3 was being or had been committed.

M.Whichell

Signature

| S | 4 | 8 | 1 | | 1 |

Traffic Warden or
Police Constable Number

PAYMENT

If before the end of 21 days from the date of this
notice the sum of £6 (being the fixed penalty for
the offence) is paid to the Chief Clerk, Fixed Penalty
Office, 185 Marylebone Road, London NW1 5QU,
the Police will not take proceedings for the offence
and any person's liability to conviction of the
offence will be discharged.

The person paying the fixed penalty must forward
with the remittance Part 2 of this notice or identify
this notice by quoting its serial number.

NOTE: IT IS AN OFFENCE FOR ANYONE OTHER
THAN THE PERSON LIABLE FOR THE ABOVE
MENTIONED OFFENCE OR THE DRIVER OR THE
PERSON IN CHARGE OF THE VEHICLE OR ANY
PERSON AUTHORISED BY ANY SUCH PERSON
TO REMOVE OR INTERFERE WITH THIS NOTICE.

405 7921 4

Put your headlights on!

'Hey, put your headlights on,' Nately shouted. 'And watch the road!'

'They are on. Isn't Yossarian in this car? That's the only reason I let the rest of you bastards in.' Chief White Halfoat turned completely around to stare into the back seat.

'Watch the road!'

'Yossarian? Is Yossarian in here?'

'I'm here, Chief. Let's go home. What makes you so sure? You never answered my question.'

'You see? I *told* you he was here.'

'What question?'

'Whatever it was we were talking about.'

'Was it important?'

'I don't remember if it was important or not. I wish to God I knew what it was.'

'There is no God.'

'*That's* what we were talking about,' Yossarian cried. 'What makes you so sure?'

'Hey, are you sure your headlights are on?' Nately called out.

'They're on, they're on. What does he want from me? It's all this rain on the windshield that makes it look dark from back there.'

'Beautiful, beautiful rain.'

'I hope it never stops raining. Rain, rain go a—'

'—way. Come a—'

'—gain some oth—'

'er day. Little Yo-Yo wants—'

'—to play. In—'

'—the meadow, in—'

Chief White Halfoat missed the next turn in the road and ran the jeep all the way up to the crest of a steep embankment. Rolling back down, the jeep turned over on its side and settled softly in the mud. There was a frightened silence.

'Is everyone all right?' Chief White Halfoat inquired in a hushed voice. No one was injured, and he heaved a long sigh of relief. 'You know, that's my trouble,' he groaned. 'I never listen to anybody. Somebody kept telling me to put my headlights on, but I just wouldn't listen.'

'I kept telling you to put your headlights on.'

'I know, I know. And I just wouldn't listen, would I? I wish I had a drink. I *do* have a drink. Look. It's not broken.'

'It's raining in,' Nately noticed. 'I'm getting wet.'

Chief White Halfoat got the bottle of rye open, drank and handed it off. Lying tangled up on top of each other, they all drank but Nately, who kept groping ineffectually for the door handle. The bottle fell against his head with a clunk, and whiskey poured down his neck. He began writhing convulsively.

'Hey, we've got to get out of here!' he cried. 'We'll all drown.'

(Joseph Heller, *Catch-22*)

crest: top
embankment: earth wall at the side of the road
hushed: quiet
heaved a . . . sigh of relief: breathed out noisily, showing relief
rye: a kind of whisky

tangled up: mixed up
groping: feeling blindly
ineffectually: uselessly, unsuccessfully
clunk: a noise
writhing convulsively: twisting his body violently

Rallying

Lancias unleash power in drive through Alps

Monte Carlo, Jan 20.—Italian Lancias held a strong grip on the 4,800-kilometre (3,000-mile) Monte Carlo Rally today as 126 surviving teams tackled a 36-hour drive through the Alps. In the lead after two of the 12 second-stage speed tests, was Sandro Munari, of Italy, in the first of the sleek green-and-white Lancia Stratos, chasing his third win since 1972.

He was 1min 14sec clear of Jean-Claude Andruet, of France, in an Alpine Renault, who was involved in a non-stop battle for second place with Bjorn Waldegaard, of Sweden, in the second Stratos. Waldegaard has won the rally twice.

Andruet, a winner in 1973, was the only driver able to compete on level terms with the 260 kph (180 mph) Lancias, which revelled in the dry conditions, where their enormous power could be used

to the full. The fourth-placed Guy Frequelin, of France, in a Porsche Carrera, was 2:53 behind after the first two special sections, and Bernard Darniche, of France, driving a works-assisted Stratos, inherited fifth place, 3:04 adrift, when his compatriot, Jean-Luc Therier, crashed immediately after the second run.

Lancia were the first large works team to be affected by mechanical problems. Their third car, driven by Rafaele Pinto, was firing on only five cylinders and picked up a three-minute road penalty, dropping it a long way down the placings. In the view of most of their rivals, only mechanical incidents or accidents can stop the Lancias winning if the weather stays fine.

" Only a real blizzard would give us a chance of staying with them ", Timo Makinen, of Finland, said.

(*The Times*)

unleash: liberate
sleek: with smooth lines
revelled in: loved

works: car manufacturer
blizzard: snow-storm

Driving on ice

Competitors in this year's Monte Carlo Rally drove 2,000 miles across Europe in what should have been the toughest conditions of the winter and found just three miles of snow and ice. But British entrants returned to find much of the country paralysed.

Perhaps because we so seldom get really bad weather, British drivers seem to be caught out by ice and snow. Few have developed skill at driving on a treacherous surface and only a small proportion carry the extras which are essential equipment to the Scandinavian or Swiss.

But there are some simple rules which can ease the terrors of sub-zero motoring. The first is to make sure you can see. Sounds obvious, but it is really astounding how many drivers pull away on a frosty morning without removing the ice or snow from all windows.

Setting out on a journey, try to allow plenty of time for hold-ups and a lower average speed. Drive as smoothly as you can, with a feather touch on accelerator, brake and clutch (that will save you petrol too).

It's especially important to think ahead and try to anticipate danger situations. Ask yourself, if that truck ahead were to catch some black ice and spin across the road, would I have enough room to take avoiding action?

And if *you* start to slide, take corrective action gently and don't saw at the wheel so that you over-correct. Of course, it's a technique which you can develop only with practice. If you can get on an open space like an old airfield or some private land and push the car around until it starts to break away you will quickly learn fine control.

(Frank Page, *The Observer Review*)

caught out: taken by surprise
treacherous surface: surface that cannot be trusted
pull away: start driving
black ice: invisible ice
saw at the wheel: turn the steering-wheel violently
break away: start sliding

The weather song

January brings the snow,
Makes your feet and fingers glow.

February's ice and sleet
Freeze the toes right off your feet.

Welcome March with wintry wind,
Would thou wert not so unkind.

April brings the sweet spring showers,
On and on for hours and hours.

Farmers fear unkindly May,
Frost by night and hail by day.

June just rains and never stops,
Thirty days and spoils the crops.

In July the sun is hot.
Is it shining? No it's not.

August, cold and dank and wet
Brings more rain than any yet.

Bleak September's mist and mud
Is enough to chill the blood.

Then October adds a gale,
Wind and slush and rain and hail.

Dark November brings the fog,
Should not do it to a dog.

Freezing wet December, then
Bloody January again!

Donald Swann and Michael Flanders

sleet: mixture of rain and snow
would thou wert not so unkind: (Shakespearean English) I wish you were not so unkind
dank: cold and damp
bleak: cold and windy

Traditional sayings about the weather

Red sky at night: shepherd's delight.
Red sky in the morning: shepherd's warning.

Rain before seven, fine before eleven.

Rain, rain, go away
Come again another day.

It's raining, it's pouring
The old man's snoring.

(Sung by children in a thunderstorm)

"Right! Now I want each of you to describe the weather in your own words."

Thelwell

The weather

This is the most important topic in the land. Do not be misled by memories of your youth when, on the Continent, wanting to describe someone as exceptionally dull, you remarked: 'He is the type who would discuss the weather with you.' In England this is an ever-interesting, even thrilling topic, and you must be good at discussing the weather.

Examples for conversation

For good weather
   'Lovely day, isn't it?'
   'Isn't it *beautiful*?'
   'The sun. . . .'
   'Isn't it gorgeous?'
   'Wonderful, isn't it?'
   'It's so nice and hot. . . .'
   'Personally, I think it's so nice when it's hot – isn't it?'
   'I adore it – don't you?'

For bad weather

　'Nasty day, isn't it?'

　'Isn't it dreadful?'

　'The rain . . . I hate rain. . . .'

　'I don't like it at all. Do you?'

　'Fancy such a day in July. Rain in the morning, then a bit of sunshine, and then rain, rain, rain, all day long.'

　'I remember exactly the same July day in 1936.'

　'Yes, I remember too.'

　'Or was it in 1928?'

　'Yes, it was.'

　'Or in 1939?'

　'Yes, that's right.'

Now observe the last few sentences of this conversation. A very important rule emerges from it. You must never contradict anybody when discussing the weather. Should it hail and snow, should hurricanes uproot the trees from the sides of the road, and should someone remark to you: 'Nice day, isn't it?' – answer without hesitation: 'Isn't it lovely?'

　Learn the above conversations by heart. If you are a bit slow in picking things up, learn at least one conversation, it would do wonderfully for any occasion.

　If you do not say anything else for the rest of your life, just repeat this conversation, you still have a fair chance of passing as a remarkably witty man of sharp intellect, keen observation and extremely pleasant manners.

(George Mikes, *How To Be an Alien*)

Weather forecast

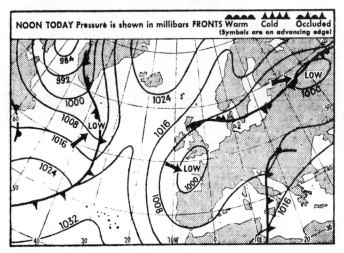

NOON TODAY Pressure is shown in millibars FRONTS Warm ▲▲▲▲ Cold ▲▲▲▲ Occluded
(Symbols are on advancing edge)

Today

Sun rises : 6.59 am   Sun sets : 5.30 pm

Moon rises : 8.56 am   Moon sets : 11.39 pm

First quarter : February 26.
Lighting up : 6.0 pm to 6.27 am.
High water : London Bridge, 4.45 am, 7.1m (23.4ft) ; 5.11 pm, 7.0m (23.0ft). Avonmouth. 10.15 am, 12.5m (41.0ft) ; 10.21 pm, 12.1m (39.6ft). Dover. 1.47 am, 6.6m (21.6ft) ; 2.8 pm, 6.2m (20.4ft). Hull, 9.10 am, 6.7m (22.0ft) ; 9.12 pm, 6.8m (22.4ft). Liverpool, 2.5 am, 8.6m (28.1ft) ; 2.18 pm, 8.6m (28.4ft).

Pressure will be low to the SW of the British Isles, with a NE airstream over most parts.

Forecasts for 6 am to midnight :
London, SE England, East Anglia : Bright or sunny intervals, showers ; wind S to SE, light or moderate ; max temp 9°C (48°F).
Central S, SW England, Channel Islands, S Wales : Bright intervals, showers ; wind E to NE, moderate ; **max temp 9°C (48°F).**
Midlands, E, Central N England : Bright intervals, showers ; wind NE, moderate ; max temp 8°C (46°F).

N Wales, NW, NE England, Lake District, Isle of Man : Mostly cloudy, rain in places, sleet on hills ; wind NE, fresh ; max temp 5° to 7°C (41° to 45°F).

Borders, Edinburgh, Dundee, SW Scotland, Glasgow, N Ireland : Mostly cloudy, perhaps brighter later, rain in places, sleet on hills ; wind NE, fresh or strong ; max temp 5° to 7°C (41° to 45°F).

Aberdeen, Central Highlands, Moray Firth, NE Scotland: Bright intervals, scattered showers, wintry on hills ; wind NE, fresh or strong ; max temp 5°C (41°F).

Argyll, NW Scotland: Bright or sunny intervals, scattered showers, wintry on hills ; wind NE, fresh or strong ; max temp 7°C (45°F).

Orkney, Shetland: Bright or sunny intervals, scattered showers, wintry in places ; wind NE, fresh or strong ; max temp 3°C (37°F).

Outlook for tomorrow and Friday: Bright intervals and showers, also longer outbreaks of rain in places ; rather cold in N, temp near normal in S.

Sea Passages: S North Sea,

Strait of Dover, English Channel (E): Wind S, moderate ; sea slight.

St George's Channel, Irish Sea: Wind NE, moderate or fresh ; sea moderate.

(*The Times*)

front: boundary between masses of cold and warm air
occluded: meeting of warm and cold front
first quarter: one of the moon's phases
lighting up time: time when cars, etc., must have their lights on

TV weather forecast

And now the weather. Apart from some cloud and rain in the South-West at first tomorrow, much of England, Wales and Northern Ireland will have sunny periods with showers chiefly in the North and East, where some will turn wintry later, but sleet or snow showers will be frequent in Northern and Eastern Scotland. It'll be much colder and windier tomorrow, with temperatures ranging from 3° centigrade (37° fahrenheit) in Northern Scotland, to 9° centigrade (48° fahrenheit) in South-West England. And that's the weather for tomorrow.

(BBC TV)

For sale at £12: Accurate Aneroid Barometer; owner too depressed to read it.

(Reading *Mercury*)

Rivers, seas and oceans

Nearly three-quarters of the Earth is covered with water. Water heats up more slowly than land, but once it has become warm it takes longer to cool down. If the Earth's surface were entirely land, the temperature at night would fall quite quickly and night would be much colder than day, as it is on the moon. This does indeed happen in inland deserts, hundreds of miles from any sea. The climate of the continents, especially in the temperate zones, is very much affected by the oceans around them. The areas close to the sea have a 'maritime climate', with rather cool summers and warm winters. The interiors, far from the sea, have a 'continental climate' with extremely hot summers and cold winters.

Rain comes from the evaporation of rivers, seas and lakes. Even after heavy rain, the pavements in a city do not take long to dry because the rainwater evaporates into the air. On a warm dry day it evaporates very rapidly, as warm air can absorb more moisture than cold air. But at any particular temperature, the atmosphere can hold only a certain maximum amount of water vapour. The air is then saturated, like a sponge that cannot hold any more water. The lower the temperature, the less water vapour is required to saturate the air.

All over the surface of the Earth, millions of tons of water are evaporating every second, condensing in the air into drops so small that it takes thousands of them to make a single raindrop. It is these tiny droplets that make clouds. When clouds roll in from the sea over the warmer land, they are forced to rise and become cooler in the colder upper atmosphere. As the air cools down it may pass through its saturation point and then some of its water vapour turns to rain. Day in, day out, the same water circulates between the air and the land: rivers evaporate to make clouds, clouds make rain, rain makes rivers which in turn run into the sea. This is called the rain cycle.

(*Penguin Book of the Physical World*)

temperate zones: parts of the world which are neither very hot nor very cold
evaporation: changing from liquid to gas
vapour: water in the form of steam or gas

'I'm afraid it's the weather'

Dear mum
in having a lovely
time we got
went out for
a walk but
a blizard of
hailstones
made us go back
Love Thomas
!
. Michel.

A Dickinson Robinson Group Company

Mrs H.A. Swan
37 Hill Top Road
Oxford.

Snowdon from Crib Goch
A view towards the snow-clad summit of the Snowdon range from the top of Crib Goch, one of the
ridges which radiate from the centre formed by the
Snowdon peak

Printed in Great Britain by J ARTHUR DIXON LTD

(Postcard from a child on holiday in the mountains)

blizard: (correct spelling *blizzard*) storm of snow or hail

157

The story of Noah

This is the story of Noah. Noah was a righteous man, the one blameless man of his time; he walked with God. He had three sons, Shem, Ham and Japheth. Now God saw that the whole world was corrupt and full of violence. In his sight the world had become corrupted, for all men had lived corrupt lives on earth. God said to Noah, 'The loathsomeness of all mankind has become plain to me, for through them the earth is full of violence. I intend to destroy them, and the earth with them. Make yourself an ark with ribs of cypress. . . . I intend to bring the waters of the flood over the earth to destroy every human being under heaven that has the spirit of life, everything on earth shall perish. But with you I shall make a covenant, and you shall go into the ark, you and your sons, your wife and your sons' wives with you. And you shall bring living creatures of every kind into the ark to keep them alive with you, two of every kind, a male and a female; two of every kind of bird, beast and reptile shall come to you to be kept alive. . . .' Noah did all that the LORD had commanded him. He was six hundred years old when the waters of the flood came upon the earth. . . . In the years when Noah was six hundred years old, on the seventeenth day of the second month, on that very day, all the springs of the great abyss broke through, the windows of the sky were opened, and rain fell on the earth for forty days and forty nights. . . . The flood continued upon the earth for forty days, and the waters swelled and lifted up the ark so that it rose high above the ground. They swelled and increased over the earth, and the ark floated on the surface of the waters. More and more the waters increased over the earth until they covered all the high mountains everywhere under heaven. The waters increased and the mountains were covered to a depth of fifteen cubits. Every living creature that moves on earth perished, birds, cattle, wild animals, all reptiles, and all mankind. Everything died that had the breath of life in its nostrils, everything on dry land. God wiped out every living thing that existed on earth, man and beast, reptile and bird; they were all wiped out over the whole earth, and only Noah and his company in the ark survived.

(Genesis 6–7, *New English Bible*)

righteous: good, moral
corrupt: bad, immoral
loathsomeness: horrible, disgusting character
ark: boat
cypress: a tree
covenant: agreement
abyss: very deep hole
cubit: old measure, around 20 inches (50 cm)

"*Good grief, it's the wife!*"

(*Punch Book of Travel*)

Dear God,
Last week it rained three days.
We thought it would be
like Noah's ark but
it wasn't. I'm glad because
you could only take
two of things, remember, and
we have three cats.

Goodbye now,
Donna

DEAR GOD,
If you know so much how
come you never made
the river big enough for
all the water and our
house got flooded and
now we got to move.
                    Victor

Dear God,
Church is alright but you
could sure use better music
I hope this does not hurt
Your feeling.
Can you write some new songs

        Your friend
        Barry

Dear God,

Are boys better than girls, I know you are one but try to be fair.

Sylvia.

DEAR GOD,
I WOULD LIKE THESE THINGS.
   a new bicycle
   a number three chemistry set
   a dog
   a movie camera
   a first baseman glove
IF I CANT HAVE THEM
ALL I WOULD LIKE TO
HAVE MOST OF THEM.
              YOURS
                   TRULY,
              ERIC

P.S. I KNOW THERE IS NO
SANTA CLAUS.

(Eric Marshall and Stuart Hemple, *Children's Letters to God*)

first baseman: a position in baseball
Santa Claus: Father Christmas

Last night a Co-operative Stores official said:
'We have another Father Christmas now.
We are sorry about Mr Bates because he was
so popular with the children. But we couldn't
have him giving away toys.'

(*Daily Mail*)

Adrian Henri's talking after Christmas blues

Well I woke up this mornin' it was Christmas Day
And the birds were singing the night away
I saw my stocking lying on the chair
Looked right to the bottom but you weren't there
there was
> apples
>> oranges
>>> chocolates
>>>> . . . aftershave

– but no you.

So I went downstairs and the dinner was fine
There was pudding and turkey and lots of wine
And I pulled those crackers with a laughing face
Till I saw there was no one in your place
there was
> mincepies
>> brandy
>>> nuts and raisins
>>>> . . . mashed potato

– but no you.

Now it's New Year and it's Auld Lang Syne
And it's 12 o'clock and I'm feeling fine
Should Auld Acquaintance be Forgot?
I don't know girl, but it hurts a lot
there was
> whisky
>> vodka
>>> dry Martini (stirred
>>> but not shaken)

. . . and 12 New Year resolutions
– all of them about you.

So it's all the best for the year ahead
As I stagger upstairs and into bed
Then I looked at the pillow by my side
. . . I tell you baby I almost cried
there'll be

      Autumn
        Summer
          Spring
            . . . and Winter
– all of them without you.

Adrian Henri

Auld Lang Syne: Scottish for 'old long since' (= the old days – title of a song that is sung at New Year)
Should Auld Acquaintance be Forgot?: Should old friends be forgotten? (the first line of the song)
stagger: walk unsteadily

Thanks

Dear Uncle Arthur,

Thank you for your extremely generous Christmas present. I don't know how you guessed, but socks were *exactly* what I wanted.

What socks, too! I have looked it up and see that it is the Macpherson tartan. And how clever of you to remember that I take size seven!

Dear Aunt Millie,

How very kind of you to remember me at Christmas! And with socks, too! In fact socks were quite the nicest present I received – size ten was just right, and the very delicate mauve will go excellently with a yellow suit. I must try to get one.

Dear Mrs Thimble,

I can't tell you how touched I am that you still go on remembering us 'children' (as I suppose you still think of us!!) every year. And socks were just what I needed. I particularly like the pretty blue ribbons they do up with – they match perfectly the bluebells on the matinee jacket you gave me last Christmas. I shall certainly think of you every time I wear them.

Dear Great-Uncle Alexander

I scarcely know what to say! I must admit I had been secretly hoping that someone would give me socks – and you did! Socks are always handy.

to have – and yours were so cleverly and appropriately Christmassy. I don't think I have ever seen socks with a pattern of holly and mistletoe before, though my favourites are the 'Yuletide Lafter' pair. Some of the jokes printed on them are almost too good to keep hidden under one's trouser-leg!

Dear Great-aunt Tilly,

I must write at once to thank you for your magnificent present. I can't tell you what my feelings were when I opened that huge parcel and found it contained – a pair of socks!

It was very clever of you to choose a pair with one red and one grey. They make a great change from the ordinary run of socks, and I shall keep them for very special occasions. And how thoughtful of you to remember that my right foot is two inches longer than my left!

I hope you haven't been having any more trouble with your eyesight recently.

Dear Aunt Clara,

Socks! I scarcely know what to say! What ever should I do without my annual supply of socks from you? I suppose I ought really to thank Aunt Millie, who first put the idea into your head fifteen years ago by showing you a snapshot of me on a Boy Scout hike. Yes, as you say, a Boy Scout can always do with another pair of socks.

I was very struck by the pattern. As you know, I have distant American connections on my mother's side, so the stars and stripes motif is particularly suitable.

Dear Aunt Lou,

I scarcely know what to say! Socks! Well, what a surprise!

I'm particularly touched because I can see at a glance that they're home-knitted. You can't buy socks like that in the shops! They never manage to get the heel quite as comfortably far forward on shop-bought socks as you have, and they always make them so ridiculously tightly knit. You can suffocate a foot without plenty of air-spaces in the sock.

How did you guess I took size fifteen?

Michael Frayn

tartan: pattern used on Scottish clothes
mistletoe: plant which grows on trees, used for decoration at Christmas
'Yuletide Lafter': Christmas laughter
snapshot: photograph
hike: long walk

A Christmas carol

Hark, the herald angels sing
Glory to the new-born king.
Peace on earth and mercy mild,
God and sinners reconciled.
Hail, redemption's happy dawn,
Hail, thou ever-blessed morn;
Sing through all Jerusalem
Christ is born in Bethlehem.

hark: listen
herald: person who makes public announcements for a king
reconciled: made friends again
hail: welcome
redemption: Christian idea that man was liberated from sin by Christ's suffering and
  death

The true spirit of Christmas

It's always seemed to me, after all, that Christmas with its spirit of giving,
offers us all a wonderful opportunity each year to reflect on what we all most
sincerely and deeply believe in – I refer, of course, to money. And yet none
of the Christmas carols that you hear on the radio or in the street ever
attempts to capture the true spirit of Christmas as we celebrate it in the US –
that is to say, the commercial spirit . . .

> Hark the Herald Tribune sings
> Advertising wondrous things . . .
> Angels we have heard on high
> Tell us to go out and buy.

Tom Lehrer

CHRISTMAS IS NEARLY HERE!

££££'s AND ££££'s ARE BEING

SPENT ON CHRISTMAS PRESENTS

make sure you get your share

Why not advertise in our

Christmas Gift Guide

RING NOW ON

01-837 3311 or 01-278 9351

(Advertisement in *The Times*)

My hubby sells Christmas cards in his shop. Every year he picks one from the shelf, gives it to me – without writing on it – and then asks me to put it back when I've read it.

(Letter in *Daily Mirror*, quoted in *New Statesman*)

hubby: (slang) husband

Good King Wenceslas – a carol

Good King Wenceslas looked out
On the feast of Stephen
When the snow lay round about
Deep and crisp and even.
Brightly shone the moon that night
Though the frost was cruel
When a poor man came in sight
Gathering winter fuel.

'Hither, page, and stand by me,
If thou knowst it telling.
Yonder peasant, who is he?
Where and what his dwelling?'
'Sire, he lives a good league hence
Underneath the mountain,
Right against the forest fence,
By St Agnes' fountain.'

'Bring me flesh and bring me wine,
Bring me pine logs hither.
Thou and I shall see him dine
When we bear them thither.'
Page and monarch forth they went,
Forth they went together,
Through the rude wind's wild lament,
And the bitter weather.

'Sire the night is darker now
And the wind blows stronger.
Fails my heart, I know not how,
I can go no longer.'

'Mark my footsteps, good my page,
Tread thou in them boldly,
Thou shalt find the winter's rage
Freeze thy blood less coldly.'

In his master's steps he trod
Where the snow lay dinted.
Heat was in the very sod
Which the saint had printed.
Therefore Christian men be sure
Wealth or rank possessing,
Ye who now shall bless the poor
Shall yourselves find blessing.

hither: (come) here
page: boy servant
yonder: that, over there
league: old measure, about three miles,
nearly five kilometres
flesh: meat

logs: cut branches used for firewood
thither: there
forth: out
lament: complaining
dinted: pressed down
sod: earth

The computer's second Christmas card

```
goodk kkkkk unjam ingwe nches lass? start again goodk
lassw enche sking start again kings tart! again sorry
goodk ingwe ncesl ooked outas thef? unmix asloo kedou
tonth effff rewri tenow goodk ingwe ncesl asloo kedou
tonth effff fffff unjam feast ofsai ntste venst efanc
utsai ntrew ritef easto fstep toeso rryan dsons orry!
start again good? yesgo odkin gwenc eslas looke dout?
doubt wrong track start again goodk ingwe ncesl asloo
kedou tonth efeas tofst ephph phphp hphph unjam phphp
repea tunja mhphp scrub carol hphph repea tscru bcaro
lstop subst itute track merry chris tmasa ndgoo dnewy
earin 1699? check digit banks orryi n1966 endme ssage
```

Edwin Morgan

unjam: unstick
Steptoe and Son: characters in a television series
scrub: cancel, abandon
digit banks: number stores

Children's version

Good King Wenceslas
Knocked a bobby senseless
Right in the middle of Marks and Spencer's.

bobby: (slang) policeman

Children's rhymes

A notorious instance of the transmission of scurrilous verses occurred in 1936 at the time of the Abdication. The word-of-mouth rhymes which then gained currency were of a kind which could not possibly, at that time, have been printed, broadcast, or even repeated in the music halls. One verse, in particular, made up one can only wonder by whom,

Hark, the herald angels sing,
Mrs Simpson's pinched our king,

was on juvenile lips not only in London, but as far away as Chichester in the south, and Liverpool and Oldham in the north. News that there was a constitutional crisis did not become public property until around 25 November of that year, and the king abdicated on 10 December. Yet at a school Christmas party in Swansea given before the end of term, Christmas 1936, when the tune played happened to be 'Hark, the herald angels sing', a mistress found herself having to restrain her small children from singing this lyric, known to all of them, which cannot have been composed much more than three weeks previously. Many an advertising executive with a six-figure budget at his disposal might envy such crowd penetration.

(Iona and Peter Opie, *The Lore and Language of Schoolchildren*)

scurrilous: insulting
Abdication: resignation of a king (in 1936, King Edward VIII abdicated because he wished to marry a woman, Mrs Simpson, who had been divorced)
gained currency: became popular
juvenile: young
with a six-figure budget at his disposal: with hundreds of thousands of pounds to spend
crowd penetration: effective communication to large numbers of people

The Press and Royalty

Let's look at the character of each British newspaper each covering the same story. Let us imagine that Princess Anne married a coloured man, say an African goat-herder.

Morning Star

MARRIAGE OF CONVENIENCE CUNNING MOVE BY HEATH GOVERNMENT TO PLACATE BLACK RHODESIANS

Sun

IT'S A WHITE AND BLACK WEDDING FOR ANNE

Financial Times

Sound financial move by Royal Family

The forthcoming marriage of Princess Anne to a native Rhodesian commoner will entitle her to £100,000 from the privy purse as a married woman. Her husband's goat herd will be put in her name. The goats will go public next year as Royal Goat Herd (Holdings) Limited.

Private Eye

PRINCESS ANNE REQUESTS PERMISSION TO MARRY WOG SHEPHERD, OPTICIAN ROYAL CALLED TO PALACE

No more coloured TV for her, says Angry Philip. When the Royal parents were informed of their daughter's wishes, the husband presumptive, a Mr N'galu N'Goolie, was rushed to Buckingham Palace where surgeons worked on him all night with powerful bleaches. This morning his condition was described as 'fair'.

Daily Telegraph

Colourful Royal Wedding

It was announced from the Palace today that Her Royal Highness is to marry Mr N'galu N'Goolie, a foreign gentleman with farming connections in Africa, his dark skin no doubt the result of long hours in the tropical sun supervising his herds.

Daily Mail

ITS HATS OFF TO ANOTHER ROYAL FIRST

Our sporting Princess is to marry a dashing dusky African goat-herder. During her recent trip, our sporting Princess fell in love with dashing 5ft. 8in. Masai N'Goolie Esq. A spokesman at the Palace said: 'They met by accident. She ran over him in a Land Rover.'

The Times

Reports are coming in from our foreign correspondent that Her Royal Highness Princess Anne is unwell. Reuter.

There is no more to say about the Press. If there is, you say it.

(*Punch*)

placate: calm down, put in a better temper
commoner: person who does not belong to a royal or noble family
privy purse: the royal family's 'salary'
go public: become a public limited company
wog: insulting word for Arab or black African
husband presumptive: future husband
bleach: chemical used for removing colour
dashing: romantic, brave
dusky: dark

Royal visit to Huddersfield

Now take this here Prince Charles. I think it's a real tragedy that lad hasn't been sent to a proper school. Just an ordinary school in a decent area, a local day school. If he mixed with the ordinary lads, he'd know summat, and they'd know summat. I don't know what they're frightened of. Are they frightened of the Royal Family knowing how we live? I remember Princess Elizabeth as she was then, coming to Huddersfield. The way they decorated it up! The way they dolled the mills up! And the way we had to go to work in special overalls that day! We weren't allowed to dirty them, we daren't do a spot of work in case we got a bit of dirt on us (mine's a filthy job, you can't work two minutes without being black all over). But no, you'd got to be bright and clean for when she saw us. Now that's all wrong. Wrong altogether! I've tried to fathom this out, but I can't study it out no way. Don't they like the way Huddersfield looks? Do they think she won't like it if she sees it? Nay, it's altogether wrong.

(A workman, quoted in Brian Jackson and Dennis Marsden, *Education and the Working Class*)

lad: boy
summat: (dialect) something
dolled up: made pretty
fathom out: get to understand

Prince Charles, aged 18, passed his driving test first bash yesterday. He went through the 45-minute exam at Isleworth, Middlesex, in a special car with a special examiner over a special route. Apart from that it was quite normal.

(*Daily Sketch*)

first bash: (slang) at the first attempt

COURT
CIRCULAR

BUCKINGHAM PALACE
November 24 : The Queen, accompanied by The Duke of Edinburgh and The Princess Anne, Mrs Mark Phillips, went in State to the Palace of Westminster to-day to open the Session of Parliament.

The Royal Procession was formed in the following order :

The Irish State Coach
(Six Grey Horses)
HER MAJESTY THE QUEEN
HIS ROYAL HIGHNESS THE
PRINCE PHILIP,
DUKE OF EDINBURGH
Second Carriage
(The Scottish State Coach with Four Grey Horses)
Her Royal Highness
The Princess Anne,
Mrs Mark Phillips
The Duke of Beaufort
(Master of the Horse)
Third Carriage
(State Landau with Two Bay Horses)
The Duchess of Grafton (Mistress of the Robes)
The Duke of Northumberland (Lord Steward)
Fourth Carriage
(State Landau with Two Bay Horses)
The Countess of Cromer (Lady in Waiting)
Mrs John Dugdale (Lady in Waiting)

Field Marshal Sir Gerald Templer (Gold Stick in Waiting)
Fifth Carriage
(State Landau with Two Bay Horses)
Admiral Sir Nigel Henderson (Vice-Admiral of the United Kingdom)
The Lord Hamilton of Dalzell (Lord in Waiting)
Lieutenant-Colonel the Right Hon. Sir Martin Charteris (Private Secretary)
Major Sir Rennie Maudslay (Keeper of the Privy Purse)
Sixth Carriage
(State Landau with Two Bay Horses)
Mr Walter Harrison, MP (Treasurer of the Household)
Mr Joseph Harper, MP (Comptroller of the Household)
Lieutenant-Commander Anthony Blackburn, RN (Equerry to The Duke of Edinburgh)
Seventh Carriage
(State Landau with Two Bay Horses)
Colonel James Eyre (Silver Stick in Waiting)
Colonel M. P. de Klee (Field Officer in Brigade Waiting)
Major Robin Broke (Equerry in Waiting)
Motor Car
Lieutenant-Colonel Sir John Miller (Crown Equerry)

Court Circular: document issued by the palace with information about the royal family's official and social life
in State: with full ceremony
landau: kind of coach
bay: reddish-brown
in waiting: in attendance on the Queen
equerry: personal assistant

Summons for Princess

The Chief Constable of Derbyshire revealed
yesterday that Princess Anne had been served
with a summons alleging speeding. She was
driving on the M1 motorway on 27 November,
accompanied by her husband, Captain Mark
Phillips, when she was stopped by a police car.

(Newspaper report)

summons: paper ordering a person to go to court
alleging: accusing her of

'Pussy cat, pussy cat, where have you been?'
'I've been to London to see the Queen.'
'Pussy cat, pussy cat, what did you there?'
'I caught a little mouse under her chair.'

(Traditional children's nursery rhyme)

'Pussy cat, pussy cat, where have you been?'
'I've been to London to visit the Queen.'
'Pussy cat, pussy cat, what did she say?'
'Something beginning "My Husband and I . . .".'

R. A. Peacock

From the Queen's speech to Parliament

The Queen opened the new session of Parliament this morning. The Queen's Speech was as follows:

My Lords and Members of the House of Commons

My husband and I look forward to the events being prepared to mark the twenty-fifth anniversary of my accession to the Throne. We welcome the opportunities which these will offer for meeting people in many parts of the United Kingdom and the Commonwealth during the tours which we shall undertake.

My Government will maintain their firm support for the United Nations and the principles of its charter, and for the North Atlantic Alliance as the guarantee of the collective security of its members and of stability between East and West. They have invited the North Atlantic Council to hold its spring ministerial meeting in London.

My Government look forward to a renewal of fruitful exchanges on world problems at the meeting of Commonwealth Heads of Government in London.

My Government will continue to take part in international efforts to promote a more stable world economic order, and a fairer distribution, within an expanding world economy, of the world's wealth between rich and poor nations. Overseas aid will continue to give increasing emphasis to the needs of the poorest developing countries.

(*The Times*)

my accession to the Throne: my becoming Queen
charter: document setting out guiding principles

*"If our prayers are answered, my son, and you
become a queen, see me after the game."*

(*Punch*)

queen: (1) the most powerful piece in chess, (2) homosexual

A chess problem

[The English names of the chess pieces are King, Queen, Bishop, Knight,
Castle (or Rook), Pawns. Solution on page 178.]

Solution on page 178.

BELKADI

(Siegen, 1970)

Black to play and win

BARRIERA

(Alexander, *Penguin Book of Chess Positions*)

Solution to chess problem on page 177

1. . . . B–B4!; 2.Resigns. If 2.Q×B then 2. . . . Q–K8mate,
and otherwise White loses the Queen. Ideas – pin and over-
load. The expert notices two things at once: (*a*) the K and Q
on the same diagonal, and (*b*) that the White Queen must
prevent Q–K8mate. You can, if you like, call it a decoy combination with the White Queen drawn away from its main task
to capture the Bishop; but I think the best way to look at it is
to think of the Queen as overloaded – it just has too much
to do after 1. . . . B–B4.

(Alexander, *Penguin Book of Chess Positions*)

. . . . *B–B4!:* the black bishop moves to the fourth square on the bishop's file (= the
line where the bishop stands at the beginning of the game); the exclamation mark
indicates that it is a good move
$Q \times B$: the white queen takes the bishop
pin: put a piece in a position where it cannot move without putting another piece in
danger
decoy: attract away

SPORTS

(The box-office number for Madison Square
Garden, Eighth Ave. between 31st and 33rd
Sts., is 564-4400, and for the Nassau Coliseum,
Hempstead Turnpike, Uniondale, L.I., 516
794-9100.)

AUTOMOBILE RACING—United States Grand Prix.
(Watkins Glen. Sunday, Oct. 10, at 2:15.)

BASEBALL—AMERICAN LEAGUE CHAMPIONSHIP PLAY-
OFFS: Yankees vs. Kansas City. The first two
games will be played in Kansas City, Saturday and Sunday, Oct. 9-10, and the third
and, if necessary, the fourth and fifth games
at Yankee Stadium, Tuesday, Oct. 12, at
8:15; Wednesday, Oct. 13, at 3:15; and
Thursday, Oct. 14, at 8:15. . . . WORLD SERIES:
Starts Saturday, Oct. 16, in the home park
of the National League champion.

PROFESSIONAL BASKETBALL—Exhibition games at
Madison Square Garden: Knicks vs. Nets,
Thursday, Oct. 7, at 7:30. . . . ¶ Philadelphia
vs. Boston and Knicks vs. Washington,
Thursday, Oct. 14, at 6. . . . ¶ Philadelphia
vs. Washington and Boston vs. Knicks, Saturday, Oct. 16, at 6.

COLLEGE FOOTBALL—SATURDAY, OCT. 9 (all games
at 1:30): Brown vs. Pennsylvania, at Provi-
dence. . . . ¶ Colgate vs. Holy Cross, at Hamilton. . . . ¶ Columbia vs. Princeton, at Baker

Field. . . . ¶ Harvard vs. Cornell, at Cambridge. . . . ¶ Rutgers vs. Connecticut, at New Brunswick. . . . ¶ Williams vs. Trinity, at Williamstown. . . . ¶ Yale vs. Dartmouth, at New Haven. . . . SATURDAY, OCT. 16: Cornell vs. Brown, at Ithaca, at 1:30. . . . ¶ Dartmouth

(*New Yorker*)

box-office: ticket-office
vs.: versus (= against)

Meads was kicked on the head, and had to have three stitches put in the cut. Kirkpatrick broke his nose early in the match. Villepreux played most of the game with two ribs broken. Many others were hurt. Some of the injuries were deliberately inflicted. These deeds made unpleasant watching. But, taken as a whole, this was not a game that got out of hand.

(*Guardian*)

out of hand: out of control

Talking about football

[This is a transcription of part of a tape-recorded conversation between three people (A, B and C). The text is specially marked so as to show those elements of spoken language which are usually lost when a conversation is written down – intonation, stress, and rhythm, noises of hesitation and agreement, etc. The meaning of the signs is as follows:

| : boundary between tone-units
| : first stressed syllable in a tone-unit
` ´ – ˇ : falling, rising, level and falling-rising tones
' : stressed syllable
↑ : stressed, high-pitched syllable
· – – – : pauses of different lengths
capital letters : word with strongest stress in a tone-unit]

A well |what's the · |what's the 'failure with the ↑FÒOTBALL| I
   mean |this · |this I don't 'really ↑SÈE| I mean it · |cos the
   ↑MÒNEY| · |how 'much does it 'cost to get ÌN| |down the ↑RÒAD|
   |NÒW|

B   I |think it ↑probably – it|
   |probably 'is the ↑MÒNEY| for |what you ↑GÈT| you |KNÓW| – erm
   I was |reading in the ↑paper this ↑MÒRNING| a a |CHÀP| he's a
   DI|RÈCTOR| of a |big ↑CÒMPANY| in |BÌRMINGHAM| – who was th
   the |world's ↑number 'one ↑FÒOTBALL 'fan| he |used to ↑SPÈND|
   a|bout a 'thousand a ↑YÈAR| |watching FÒOTBALL| you |KNÓW|
   (C: |CÒO|) – he's he's |watched 'football in ↑every n · on
   ↑every 'league · 'ground in ÉNGLAND| |all 'ninety TWÓ|
   (A laughs) – and he's |been to A↑MĒRICA| to |watch ↑West
   BRŌMWICH 'playing in A'merica| he's · he's |been to the la
   · to |ÒH| · the |LÀST| f f |two or 'three 'world CÙP| · |world
   CÙP| · mat |THÍNGS| you |KNÓW| · |TÓURNAMENTS| – – and he |goes
   to ↑all the 'matches AWÁY| you |KNÓW| |European ↑CÙP 'matches
   and 'everything| that |ÈNGLISH teams are PLÁYING in| he's all
   'over the ↑WÒRLD 'watching it you SÉE| – |THÌS YÉAR| he's

|watched ↑twenty 'two GÀMES| – |SÒ 'far| |this YÈAR| which is
a|bout · FÌFTY per 'cent| of his |NŎRMAL| (C: |good LÒRD|) · and
|even ↑HÈ's getting 'browned ↑ÓFF| and |HÈ was SÁYING| that
erm – you can |go to a NÍGHTCLUB| in |BĬRMINGHAM| – – and
|watch ↑Tony BÉNNET| · for a|bout ↑thirty ↑BŌB| – |something
like THÍS| a |night with ↑Tony ↑BÉNNET| – |have a 'nice ↑MĒAL|
· in · |very · ↑plushy SURRŌUNDINGS| very |WĀRM|
|NÍCE| |PLÈASANT| – says it |CÒSTS him| a|bout the ↑SÀME
a'mount of MÓNEY| to |go and ↑sit in a ↑breezy 'windy STÁND| –
(A & C *laugh*) on a · on a |WÒODEN BÉNCH| – to |WĂTCH| a |rather
BÓRING 'game of ↑FÒOTBALL| with |no ↑PERSONÁLITY| and |all
DEFÉNSIVE| and |ÈVERYTHING| he |says it's just ↑KÌLLING itself|
you |KNÓW| (A: |YÈAH| C: |M̌|) – they're |not 'giving the
'enter'tainment they ÚSED to 'give| the erm – CON|DÌTIONS have|
if |ÀNYTHING| are |not are f DE|TĚRIORATED| and er (C: in |what
WÀY|) they're |charging f ↑three 'times what they ↑ÙSED to| ·
or |four 'times what they ↑ÙSED to|

(Crystal and Davy, *Advanced Conversational English*)

cos: because
to get in down the road: to get in to see a football match at the local ground
fan: enthusiast
coo: exclamation
browned off: (slang) fed up
thirty bob: (slang) thirty shillings, i.e. £1.50
plushy: luxurious
deteriorated: got worse

Cardiff City v. Tottenham Hotspur

... and so it's Cardiff City in the dark blue strips who kick off ... that's Giles ... that's Evans ... Keith Osgood wearing number 6 ... Littlemore in there challenging ...

... throw again for Tottenham ...

... goal kick ... that's Coates ... good ball, a good chance – it's a goal! A beautiful ball through by Peter Evans and then Sayer number 10, makes it one goal to nil for Cardiff.

... and Osgood trying to find ... and almost got through ... Steve Gorman with the interception ... away by Dwyer ...

... now it's Keith Osgood – and Spurs are really keeping up the pressure in these last ten minutes of the first half ... neat, very neat – Evans got the return ball ... and Evans still going ... and Evans with a shot! ...

... Taylor with a cross ... Naylor coming in ... away by Dwyer ... that's Gorman, to Coates ... corner ...

... and that's the whistle for half time with Cardiff City leading by one goal to nil.

... Taylor ... free kick – two Tottenham players and another ... and it almost went in – it must have hit the post and rebounded – what a remarkable let-off ...

... one minute to go of playing time ... throw in to Cardiff City ... it's a corner – could this be the last corner of the match? ... the whistle has blown – and Cardiff City has knocked Tottenham Hotspur out of the FA cup – a great great victory by Cardiff City!

(From a commentary on BBC TV)

v.: versus (against)
kick off: give the kick that starts the game
goal kick: kick by the goalkeeper
interception: taking a pass that is meant for another player
let-off: escape from punishment, or from an unpleasant experience
FA: Football Association

why do all those fhootballers

Kiss each other on theTelly.
Theyre not married
Theyre not even
engaged,

Jason aged 6

When the kissing may—and should—stop

Footballers who kiss and cuddle and make gestures to the crowd after scoring a goal could be in trouble if a recommendation of the FA match and ground committee is accepted. The proposal, put to the executive and disciplinary committee, states that players who act in such a way should be charged with bringing the game into disrepute.

We all tend to fall into bad habits—by habit. With endless repetition we take matters for granted. This has been the case of the embracing footballer. Once upon a time it was never so. A few congratulatory pats on the back by his colleagues was all that the scorer of a goal once received in salute.

In the last 20 years or so, however, the fashion of hugging, squeezing and even kissing to excess the hero of the moment has grown to nauseating proportions—nauseating, that is, to people who have been able to stand back from events and avoided being brainwashed into accepting such events as part of an overall pattern. Schoolmasters in general have always been highly critical, rightly so, of these gross antics.

Sadly television—no doubt unconsciously or because it was unavoidable—has helped to highlight such moments of exaggerated euphoria in slow motion playback and endless repetition the goal of the hour, the goal of the day, the month, the year, the century and so on. There is no end to it.

(Geoffrey Green, *The Times*)

cuddle: put their arms round each other
nauseating: sickening
these gross antics: this ridiculous and disgusting behaviour
euphoria: great happiness

A 32-YEAR-OLD housewife, Dorothy Pearson, was fined £15 and bound over for a year by York magistrates for conduct likely to cause a breach of the peace during a match between York City and Tranmere. She had leaped on to the pitch when York took the lead and kissed the scorer. Mickey Cave. ' I was overcome with emotion,' she told the magistrates. ' York City don't score very often.'

(*The Observer*)

bound over for a year: warned that she would be severely punished if she committed the same offence again within a year
conduct likely to cause a breach of the peace: literally, behaviour which could lead to a public disturbance
pitch: football field

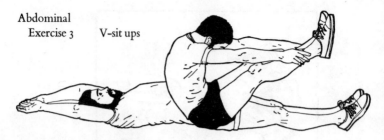

Abdominal Exercise 3	V–sit ups

Purpose
To develop strength and trim the mid section

Start
Back lying, hands reaching backwards behind the head, toes pointed

Movement
Swing into the V–sit position by lifting trunk and legs together so that you balance on both hips. Reach for the ankles with both hands

Repetitions
8 to 12 times; progress over the weeks to 15 to 30 times or more. If you wish to exceed 30 times take a 30 second pause, continue for the additional repetitions

(Carruthers and Murray, *F/40: Fitness on Forty Minutes a Week*)

trim: slim
trunk: the main part of the body

"*Quite honestly, I don't know why you bother.*"

How much faster can they go?

The 5,000 metre race at a recent international meeting in Kiev was won by
Tony Simmons of Great Britain in 13 minutes 21.2 seconds. Simmons is not
necessarily Britain's best at the distance – other contenders didn't run
because their Olympic training schedules would have been upset – and yet
if he had run at this speed before 1966 he would have broken a world record.
And if the unbeatable Paavo Nurmi had run in the same race at the speed at
which he established *his* world record in 1924, he would have been a minute
and seven seconds behind – Simmons would have lapped him. What once
seemed an unapproachable athletic performance has become less, even, than
outstanding.

World records in all athletic events are broken, and we do not even
imagine that they won't be. But why should it happen? All that is involved
in running is a courageous, trained athlete, a pair of shoes and a track.
Tracks are now more consistently good than they used to be, but even so,
it cannot be a technological change that accounts for the improvement. So
what changes *have* occurred, and, as a further thought, are we reaching the
end? Is there any sign that we are approaching the limits of human ability?

Whatever the changes are, they certainly are not improvements in the
efficiency of movement. Running is so natural a movement that those who
run a lot develop the style that is most efficient for them.

So is the difference the result of better training? A couple of ideas that have
recently taken hold suggest the possibility. One starts from the fact that
middle-distance running has improved dramatically as Ethiopians and other
East Africans have taken a more prominent part in international athletics.
They often come from mountain areas, and run and train at altitude. Their
systems are adapted to getting all the oxygen they need for their running
from the thin air of the mountains, so one could reasonably expect them to be
particularly good at getting the oxygen when they compete at more normal
heights. It would seem to follow that anyone who trained for long enough at
altitude would develop this improved mechanism for handling oxygen, and
distance runners, in particular, have sometimes included altitude training in
their schedules. It may have improved their performances, but the results are
equivocal. It may be that the bodies of the Africans have changed over a
much longer period, perhaps even as a result of biological selection, than
any athlete can devote to training.

(*The Sunday Times Magazine*)

lapped: a lap is a circuit of a running track; if one runner laps another, he gets a
complete lap ahead and overtakes him
taken hold: become popular
are equivocal: can be interpreted in different ways

40 — *Love*

middle	aged
couple	playing
ten	nis
when	the
game	ends
and	they
go	home
the	net
will	still
be	be
tween	them

Roger McGough

The unloved

I am pure loneliness
   I am empty air
      I am drifting cloud.

I have no form
   I am boundless
      I have no rest.

I have no house
   I pass through places
      I am indifferent wind.

I am the white bird
   Flying away from land
      I am the horizon.

I am a wave
   That will never reach the shore.

I am an empty shell
   Cast up on the sand.

I am the moonlight
   On the cottage with no roof.

I am the forgotten dead
   In the broken vault on the hill.

I am the old man
   Carrying his water in a pail.

Kathleen Raine

boundless: unlimited
vault: tomb, stone grave

Loneliness

Do you realize that this is probably the first time in the history of man that society has been deliberately structured to alienate people? A mood of separateness, isolation, loneliness is everywhere. Only the last generation has grown up in the most isolated environment ever created: the nuclear family and television.

Last week I heard a radio talk-show in which the participants were trying to discover the reasons for so much student unrest. One person speculated that one reason may be a 'racial memory of the extended family' – that is, young people are unconsciously experiencing dissatisfaction with the lack of extended-family participation. Whether or not the explanation is valid, America certainly does suffer from a lack of full family life. One remedy for this deficiency is offered by the communal movement: a realignment and restructuring of human relations to allow for more sharing, whether it is simply a strong sense of neighborliness or the evolution of an intense and involved group marriage. In anthropological terms, the extended family consists of people related by blood and marriage ties. In communal life, it consists of unrelated people who have come together as loving friends.

Loneliness and isolation gather together in the cities, where people tend to remain cut off from one another even in the most physically crowded situations – as the rush hour on New York City's subway system so aptly and sadly illustrates. 'All the lonely people, where do they come from?' is a line in the Beatles' song, 'Eleanor Rigby'. Why ask? Just listen. They are there, all around you. The need for human contact stands out on the surface of the skin (what do people really go to church for?). Right now, if you are not alone, grasp the hand of the person on either side of you and say 'hello'. Is it a little embarrassing for you to do? Embarrassing? Do you understand what it means to be embarrassed just to hold a person's hand and greet him, be he stranger, friend, or acquaintance?

(Richard Fairfield, *Communes USA*)

alienate people: separate people from society
nuclear family: family consisting only of a couple and their children
extended family: family including aunts, uncles, grandparents, etc.
communal movement: movement to establish communes in which numbers of people live together as if in a family
realignment: reorganization

Eleanor Rigby

Moderately

Ah, look at all the lonely people.

Ah, look at all the lonely people.

Eleanor Rigby picks up the rice in the church where a wedding
has been.

Lives in a dream.

Waits at the window, wearing the face that she keeps in a jar by the
door,

Who it is for?

All the lonely people, where do they all come from?

All the lonely people, where do they all belong?

Father McKenzie, writing the words of a sermon that no one will
hear,

No one comes near.

Look at him working, darning his socks in the night when there's
nobody there,

What does he care?

All the lonely people, where do they all come from?

All the lonely people, where do they all belong?

Ah, look at all the lonely people.

Ah, look at all the lonely people.

Eleanor Rigby died in the church and was buried along with her
name.

Nobody came.

Father McKenzie, wiping the dirt from his hands as he walks from
the grave.

No one was saved.

All the lonely people, where do they all come from?

All the lonely people, where do they all belong?

John Lennon and Paul McCartney

darning: mending with wool

Old age

Why not a piece, as honest as I can make it, on Old Age? A lot of people have told us how they are enjoying—or have enjoyed—their old age. I am not one of these complacent ancients. I detest being old. I can't settle down to make the most of it—whatever that may be—but resent almost every aspect of it. There is still in me a younger man, trapped, struggling to get out. It is rather as if I were press-ganged at a stage door, dragged in to submit to *old-man make-up*, and then pushed on the stage to play an objectionable character part. For instance, I am increasingly fussy about engagements and arrangements and time-tables. Meanwhile, there is a self that is aware of all this fussiness and deplores it. This confirms my opinion that in old age we are compelled to play a bad character part, not belonging to our essential and enduring self. We are out there, facing an intimate audience, making fools of ourselves.

Anyhow, I am living at the wrong time. Had I been born even 40 or 50 years earlier, I might have enjoyed going on so long. But now, it seems to me, old age is a liability without the ghost of an asset. The ripe experience of us who are old is now not of any value. It may be we have no wisdom, but then is anybody looking for wisdom? We have no longer anything important to contribute. (But then sometimes I feel that those still in their prime haven't very much, with so many huge problems around and so many inadequate solutions.) There have been civilizations of a sort in which the aged have been expected to climb a mountain and vanish for ever in its mists and snow.

Perhaps that mountain is still
with us existing in the inner
space of our juniors, hoping to
forget us.

(J. B. Priestley, *The Times*)

piece: article
complacent: self-satisfied
detest: hate
resent: dislike and regard as unfair
press-ganged: kidnapped
deplores it: thinks it is a bad thing
liability: disadvantage
asset: advantage
in their prime: in the best part of their lives

Miss Blanche Timothy received a telegram from
the Queen yesterday – her 100th birthday. 'I
was quite surprised, until then I thought I was
only 98', she said.

(*Evening Argus*)

Warning

When I am an old woman I shall wear purple
With a red hat which doesn't go, and doesn't suit me,
And I shall spend my pension on brandy and summer gloves
And satin sandals, and say we've no money for butter.
I shall sit down on the pavement when I'm tired
And gobble up samples in shops and press alarm bells
And run my stick along the public railings
And make up for the sobriety of my youth.
I shall go out in my slippers in the rain
And pick the flowers in other people's gardens
And learn to spit.

Jenny Joseph

doesn't go: doesn't go well with the purple
gobble: eat greedily
samples: examples of something that is sold
make up for: compensate for
sobriety: calm, controlled behaviour

When you are old and grey

Brightly

Since I still appreciate you,
Let's find love while we may,
Because I know I'll hate you
When you are old and grey.
So say you love me here and now,
I'll make the most of that;
Say you love and trust me,
For I know you'll disgust me
When you're old and getting fat.

An awful debility, a lessened utility,
A loss of mobility is a strong possibility.
In all probability I'll lose my virility,
And you your fertility and desirability.
And this liability of total sterility
Will lead to hostility and a sense of futility.
So let's act with agility while we still have facility,
For we'll soon reach senility and lose the ability.

Your teeth will start to go, dear,
Your waist will start to spread.
In twenty years or so, dear,
I'll wish that you were dead.
I'll never love you then at all
The way I do today,
So please remember, when I leave in December,
I told you so in May.

Tom Lehrer

debility: weakness
utility: usefulness
virility: a man's sexual power
liability: probability
hostility: dislike
futility: pointlessness
agility: speed and skill
senility: old age

When you are old

When you are old and grey and full of sleep,
And nodding by the fire, take down this book,
And slowly read, and dream of the soft look
Your eyes had once, and of their shadows deep;
How many loved your moments of glad grace,
And loved your beauty with love false or true,
But one man loved the pilgrim soul in you,
And loved the shadows of your changing face;

And bending down beside the glowing bars,
Murmur, a little sadly, how Love fled,
And paced upon the mountains overhead,
And hid his face amid a cloud of stars.

W. B. Yeats

pilgrim: wandering, searching for an ideal

Index

Topics

Poems and songs

Cartoons